W9-CPJ-194

Teens: Cutting and Self-Injury

Peggy J. Parks

Teenage Problems

ReferencePoint
Press®

San Diego, CA

© 2015 ReferencePoint Press, Inc.
Printed in the United States

For more information, contact:
ReferencePoint Press, Inc.
PO Box 27779
San Diego, CA 92198
www.ReferencePointPress.com

LIBRARY OF CONGRESS CATALOGING-IN-PUBLICATION DATA

Parks, Peggy J., 1951–
   Teens : cutting and self-injury / by Peggy J. Parks.
     pages cm. -- (Compact research series)
   Audience: Grade 9 to 12.
   Includes bibliographical references and index.
   ISBN 978-1-60152-770-7 (hardback) -- ISBN 1-60152-770-5 (hardback) 1. Self-mutilation in adolescence--Juvenile literature. 2. Self-injurious behavior--Juvenile literature. 3. Cutting (Self-mutilation)--Juvenile literature. I. Title.
   RJ506.S44P29   2015
   616.85'82--dc23
                                           2014031630

Contents

Foreword

As modern civilization continues to evolve, its ability to create, store, distribute, and access information expands exponentially. The explosion of information from all media continues to increase at a phenomenal rate. By 2020 some experts predict the worldwide information base will double every seventy-three days. While access to diverse sources of information and perspectives is paramount to any democratic society, information alone cannot help people gain knowledge and understanding. Information must be organized and presented clearly and succinctly in order to be understood. The challenge in the digital age becomes not the creation of information, but how best to sort, organize, enhance, and present information.

ReferencePoint Press developed the *Compact Research* series with this challenge of the information age in mind. More than any other subject area today, researching current issues can yield vast, diverse, and unqualified information that can be intimidating and overwhelming for even the most advanced and motivated researcher. The *Compact Research* series offers a compact, relevant, intelligent, and conveniently organized collection of information covering a variety of current topics ranging from illegal immigration and deforestation to diseases such as anorexia and meningitis.

The series focuses on three types of information: objective single-author narratives, opinion-based primary source quotations, and facts and statistics. The clearly written objective narratives provide context and reliable background information. Primary source quotes are carefully selected and cited, exposing the reader to differing points of view, and facts and statistics sections aid the reader in evaluating perspectives. Presenting these key types of information creates a richer, more balanced learning experience.

For better understanding and convenience, the series enhances information by organizing it into narrower topics and adding design features that make it easy for a reader to identify desired content. For example, in *Compact Research: Illegal Immigration*, a chapter covering the economic impact of illegal immigration has an objective narrative explaining the various ways the economy is impacted, a balanced section of numerous primary source quotes on the topic, followed by facts and full-color illustrations to encourage evaluation of contrasting perspectives.

The ancient Roman philosopher Lucius Annaeus Seneca wrote, "It is quality rather than quantity that matters." More than just a collection of content, the *Compact Research* series is simply committed to creating, finding, organizing, and presenting the most relevant and appropriate amount of information on a current topic in a user-friendly style that invites, intrigues, and fosters understanding.

Teens: Cutting and Self-Injury at a Glance

Self-Injury Defined

Self-injury (also called self-harm, deliberate self-harm, self-mutilation, self-injurious behavior, or cutting) is defined as the intentional harming of one's body without suicidal intent.

Methods of Self-Injury

Cutting is the most common method, especially among girls; other ways teens self-injure include burning, hair pulling, bruising, and head banging.

Prevalence

An estimated 6 to 7 percent of teens self-injure regularly, and as many as 25 percent have self-injured at some point during their lives.

Who Self-Injures

Teenage boys and girls of all races and ethnicities engage in self-injury.

Warning Signs

The most obvious symptoms of self-injurious behavior are visible injuries such as cuts, scratches, burns, and/or bruises.

Causes

Experts say that no one cause is responsible for self-injurious behavior; rather, many factors are likely involved.

Risks

Self-injury can lead to permanent scarring, numbness, and even death from bleeding.

Recovery

When treated, teens can overcome the need to self-injure; therapy is an important part of treatment.

Prevention Efforts

Although few self-injury prevention programs exist, mental health specialists say that self-injury prevention should be a much larger priority than it is today.

Overview

When singer and actress Demi Lovato was sixteen years old, she appeared in photographs that were taken at Miley Cyrus's Sweet Sixteen birthday party. Lovato had been a celebrity since she was a child, so being photographed on the red carpet was not at all unusual—but one picture captured the media's attention. A smiling Lovato posed for the camera holding out the pleated skirt of her dress as though to curtsy, and a close-up showed what looked like scars on the inside of her left wrist. The entertainment world was abuzz with speculation about whether the marks were from cutting, but Lovato's publicist promptly denied it, saying the allegations were "completely false."[1] Rather, she insisted that the marks were red indentations from tight-fitting gummy bracelets that Lovato had been wearing just prior to the photo being taken.

Several years passed before Lovato publicly acknowledged that the rumors had been true: The marks on her wrist were from cutting. She gave several interviews and spoke candidly about her self-harming behavior, saying that she had started cutting when she was eleven years old. In a December 2013 interview with *Access Hollywood*, Lovato talks about her recovery from self-injury after three months of treatment. She notes that the first reaction is usually shame—both on the part of the young people injuring themselves and their families. What would be more helpful, she says, is for people to have a better understanding of the problem and a willingness to talk about it. "For some reason, it's more taboo to talk about than drugs or alcohol," Lovato says, adding that self-harm is a problem that many parents are too embarrassed to face. "You think of it as such a dark thing."[2]

A Troubling Condition

When she was interviewed Lovato spoke about the emotional pain that was at the root of her self-harming behavior, which is typical of young people who deliberately harm themselves. When asked why they do it many describe feeling overwhelmed by bottled-up stress, sadness, and anger; and they turn to self-injury in a desperate attempt to find relief. Another reason some teens cut themselves is because they feel empty or numb inside and believe that physical pain is better than feeling nothing. Ron Steingard, child psychiatrist with the mental health advocacy group Child Mind Institute, explains: "They've locked down so tightly because of whatever's going on in their lives that they feel they're incapable of feeling anything at all. So they hurt themselves in order to feel something."[3]

> **Whatever positive feelings may result from cutting are quickly replaced by feelings of shame and regret.**

After self-harming many teens feel a quick burst of relief, which is believed to be caused by endorphins (feel-good chemicals) being released in the brain. This momentary relief is short-lived, however. Whatever positive feelings may result from cutting are quickly replaced by feelings of shame and regret. The residential treatment center Timberline Knolls explains: "While self-harming may bring a momentary sense of calm and a release of tension, it's usually followed by guilt and shame and the return of painful emotions."[4]

Even though teens who self-injure are deliberately causing themselves physical pain, they are rarely suicidal. A Peoria, Illinois, teenager named Alicia Moore explains: "I didn't cut myself to try to kill myself. I cut myself to release all of this emotional pain that I felt like I couldn't handle anymore."[5] The absence of suicidal intent is one criterion for the diagnosis of what is now called non-suicidal self-injury, or NSSI. This is a new diagnosis as of May 2013, when the fifth edition of the American Psychiatric Association's *Diagnostic and Statistical Manual of Mental Disorders* (DSM-5) was released.

How Teens Harm Themselves

Mental health specialists widely agree that the method used most often for self-injury is cutting. Teens use all kinds of sharp objects to cut themselves, including razor blades, knives, scissors, or shards of broken glass—anything that can cut or scratch the skin deeply enough for the person to bleed. The style and pattern of the cutting is often very personal to the teen who cuts. Pediatrician David Rosen, who directs the Section for Teenage and Young Adult Health at the University of Michigan Health Systems, explains: "The most typical cuts are very linear, straight line, often parallel like railroad ties carved into forearm, the upper arm, sometimes the legs. Some people cut words into themselves. If they're having body image issues, they may cut the word 'fat.' If they're having trouble at school, it may be 'stupid,' 'loser,' 'failure,' or a big 'L.' Those are the things we see pretty regularly."[6]

> **Mental health specialists widely agree that the method used most often for self-injury is cutting.**

Teens use other methods to deliberately harm themselves in addition to cutting. They burn themselves with a lighter, matches, or a lit cigarette, or heat a knife blade or coat hanger until it is red-hot and then hold it on their skin. They bite their arms, legs, or hands until they break the skin and draw blood, or they pull out clumps of hair. Some teens self-injure by embedding sharp objects, such as needles, staples, pencil lead, small pieces of glass, or slivers of metal or wood, under the skin. Or they may hit themselves with a hammer, rock, or other object, or bang their heads on hard surfaces. One young woman

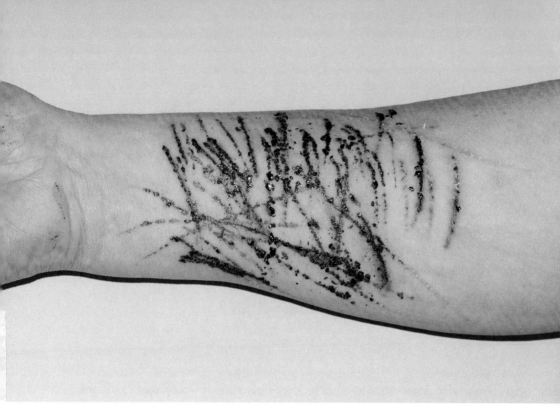

Self-inflicted lacerations appear raw and painful and are likely to leave permanent scars. Among teenagers, cutting is the most common form of self-injury.

named Emily, who intentionally bruises herself, writes: "I bruise myself rather than cut (which I used to do). I've been bruising for 2 years. The urge is there almost all the time, so intense sometimes I feel like crying."[7]

How Serious a Problem Are Cutting and Self-Injury Among Teens?

Health officials in the United States and other countries track the incidence of many diseases and disorders but not the incidence of self-injury. Thus, prevalence figures can only be compiled based on surveys of teenagers and studies conducted by researchers. As a November 2012 paper in the *Journal of the Canadian Academy of Child and Adolescent Psychiatry* explains: "Due to conflicting operational definitions for measuring self-harm . . . it is difficult to ascertain a precise prevalence rate for self-harm among clinic and community samples of adolescents. Self-harm, though, is quite prevalent in clinical samples."[8]

One expert who has extensively studied self-injury is Janis Whitlock, a research scientist and director of Cornell University's Research Program on Self-Injury and Recovery. According to Whitlock, the majority of studies conducted during the past several years have found that between 12 and 25 percent of adolescents have self-harmed at least once during their lifetimes. She adds that an estimated 6 to 7 percent of teens and young adults engage in self-harming behavior on a regular basis. In a 2013 paper Whitlock and her colleague Karen Rodham say that self-injury is widely recognized as an "all too common phenomenon among . . . populations of adolescents and young adults with important clinical, public health, and policy implications."[9]

Those Most Likely to Self-Injure

Although people of all ages have engaged in self-harming, the practice is far more common among teens than adults. This was one finding of an Australian study published in the June 2014 issue of the journal *Suicide and Life-Threatening Behavior*. The study revealed that the incidence of self-harm was 17.2 percent among adolescents, 13.4 percent among young adults, and 5.5 percent among adults.

In recent years therapists have begun to see that self-injury does not discriminate. "NSSI is both widespread and common among all kinds of youth," say Whitlock and Rodham. "High achievers, shy youth, boys and girls, popular kids, athletes."[10] In the past people assumed that only teenage girls engaged in self-harming behavior, but that has proved to be false. While it is true that research typically shows a higher prevalence among females, experts say that could be because females are much more likely than males to admit they have a problem and to seek treatment.

Warning Signs

The most telling signs that someone is self-injuring are visible injuries: cuts, severe scratches, burns, and/or bruises on the wrists, arms, legs, and/or stomach. These signs, however, are often not visible to others because many teens go out of their way to hide them from family and friends. One way they do this is to self-harm in places on their body that will not show. Or they wear long-sleeved shirts or hoodies and long pants even during the hottest summer weather and tend to become agitated when asked about it or encouraged to dress in cooler clothes. A woman named

Lily had no idea that her teenage daughter was cutting herself during the winter. But when warm, balmy spring days arrived and the girl insisted on wearing a wool sweater to school, Lily knew something was wrong. "Sandy got furious when I told her to go change," says Lily. "I've never seen her that upset! Three days of long sleeved shirts and I finally caught on. I'd heard about this, of course. But I never thought my daughter would be doing it. There are scars all up and down her arms!"[11]

Aside from visible injuries (and efforts to hide them), family members or friends may notice other signs that a teen is self-injuring. If asked about bruises, the person may use the excuse of being clumsy and often falling or bumping into things. Therapists who specialize in self-injury say that when confronted with questions about mysterious

> " **Although people of all ages have engaged in self-harming, the practice is far more common among teens than adults.** "

cuts and scratches, teens conjure up all sorts of scenarios. Typical are excuses such as they fell into a prickly brier bush or someone's cat scratched them. "I wish I had a nickel for every time someone says, 'The cat did it,'"[12] says Rosen. Other indications that teens could be self-injuring include uncharacteristic mood swings, subtle changes in personality, being quieter than usual, wanting to be alone more than usual, and/or spending long periods of time locked in their bedrooms.

What Causes Teens to Deliberately Harm Themselves?

Self-injury is a complicated disorder that experts say has no one cause. Rather, many factors are likely involved. At the root of the problem is an inability to cope in healthy ways with emotional pain, as the Mayo Clinic explains: "The person has a hard time regulating, expressing or understanding emotions. The mix of emotions that triggers self-injury is complex. For instance, there may be feelings of worthlessness, loneliness, panic, anger, guilt, rejection, self-hatred or confused sexuality."[13]

Research has shown that a common reason for the buildup of emotional pain is a family environment in which children are expected to

> **Research has shown that a common reason for the buildup of emotional pain is a family environment in which children are expected to keep negative emotions (such as sadness and anger) to themselves.**

keep negative emotions (such as sadness and anger) to themselves. In this type of family environment, the sharing of feelings and opinions is strongly discouraged and sometimes not tolerated at all. As a result, young people do not learn how to cope with feelings in a healthy way and may turn to self-injury as a way of trying to relieve their emotional tension. "Self-injury is definitely a coping strategy for unhappy kids," says psychologist and self-injury expert Wendy Lader. She goes on to describe other possible reasons for the deep emotional pain that can cause young people to turn to self-injury. "They may have a history of sexual, physical, or verbal abuse. Many are sensitive, perfectionists, overachievers. The self-injury begins as a [defense] against what's going on in their family, in their lives. They have failed in one area of their lives, so this is a way to get control."[14]

The Copycat Effect

Self-injury is typically viewed as a private, solitary behavior that most young people go out of their way to hide. But Lader and other experts are starting to see more teens who started self-harming after observing friends and acquaintances doing it, or who had become aware of it through the media. "There is sort of a contagion to this," says Lader. "Kids who are in emotional distress have heard about this from other kids or seen it on television or heard a star talk about this, and they might try it."[15]

The Internet is playing a major role in fueling the growth of self-injury among teens, with social media being especially influential. Journalist Marla Jo Fisher first became interested in the self-injury phenomenon when her daughters said many of their schoolmates were cutting themselves. She interviewed a small group of teenage girls and learned that those who self-injure often post photos on Instagram—even though self-harm imagery is prohibited under Instagram's community guidelines. The girls asked her if she wanted to see "some scars that people posted," and she told them yes. What they showed her was shocking, as she writes: "They fiddle with their phones and quickly pull up images of their classmates, arms full of scars. Photos posted online, for all to see. I wonder if their parents have any idea."[16]

Underlying Causes

Self-injury experts say that teens who harm themselves typically suffer from other mental health conditions as well. Depression is extremely common among self-injurers, as are eating disorders and anxiety disorders. Karen Conterio, who along with Lader cofounded the inpatient treatment program S.A.F.E. Alternatives, says the very fact that teens find emotional relief from self-harming is a sign of a deeper problem. "With self-injury," says Conterio, "if it works for you, that's an indication that an underlying issue needs [to] be dealt with—possibly significant psychiatric issues."[17]

> "Depression is extremely common among self-injurers, as are eating disorders and anxiety disorders."

When a teenager named Victoria Kountz was a freshman in high school, she was battling depression and says cutting gave her a sense of relief. "The first time I cut myself," she says, "it kind of distracted me from everything I was thinking and it felt like I had a sense of control." Before long Kountz became addicted to cutting, doing it an average of six times a day and carrying a blade with her most everywhere she went. "My thoughts were constantly about hurting myself,"[18] she says. The cutting became so bad that Kountz was admitted to the hospital involuntarily by her parents. With treatment she was eventually able to stop harming herself.

What Are the Risks of Cutting and Self-Injury?

Depending on the type of wounds and how severe they are, a number of physical problems may result from self-injury. The US Office on Women's Health explains: "Self-injury can be dangerous. Cutting can lead to infections, scars, numbness, and even hospitalization or death. People who share tools to cut themselves are at risk of getting and spreading diseases like HIV and hepatitis."[19]

Along with scarring, a major risk for teens who cut themselves is permanent damage to their arms and hands. According to Hamish Laing, a plastic surgeon from the United Kingdom, teens who repeatedly cut their wrists are "not very far away from the mechanics of the inside of [the] arm." Laing goes on to discuss cutting-related injuries that he often sees in his practice. "We see lots of people who have injured tendons, nerves, blood vessels and muscles. And although some of these can be repaired, if you cut a major nerve in your wrist you can be left with permanent weakness or numbness in your hand, or both. It's a very significant injury."[20]

A twenty-year-old woman named Lara started cutting herself as a teen and continued doing it for five years. Eventually, she began to notice that she was losing feeling in her left wrist. "Over a period of a few months," she says, "I completely lost feeling from my elbow down to my hand."[21]

Can Teens Overcome the Need to Self-Injure?

Teens who regularly self-injure need professional help, and with the right treatment are often able to recover. This usually involves a variety of approaches, as Mental Health America explains: "The effective treatment of self-injury is most often a combination of medication, cognitive/behavioral therapy, and interpersonal therapy, supplemented by other treatment services as needed. Medication is often useful in the management of depression, anxiety, obsessive-compulsive behaviors, and the racing thoughts that may accompany self-injury."[22]

> "Because the study of self-injury is still a young science, there are no long-term, time-tested prevention programs that have proved to be successful.

According to the Child Mind Institute, one type of therapy that is highly recommended for teens who self-injure is dialectical behavior therapy. A psychologist works closely with patients to help them learn how to tolerate uncomfortable feelings of anger, anxiety, and rejection. Over time, as the teen learns new, healthy ways of coping with

Teens who regularly self-injure can overcome their difficulties with the help of therapy and medication. Therapy can help troubled teens find healthy ways of dealing with strong emotions such as anger, anxiety, and rejection.

negative feelings, he or she will eventually stop self-harming. Child Mind Institute psychologist Jill Emanuele explains: "Many kids who engage in self-injury participate in a type of treatment called dialectical behavior therapy, or DBT for short. This therapy, among many things, teaches teens how to more effectively manage their strong emotions, without needing to resort to dangerous behaviors such as self-injury."[23]

Prevention Efforts

Because the study of self-injury is still a young science, there are no long-term, time-tested prevention programs that have proved to be successful. The Cornell University Research Program on Self-Injury and Recovery explains: "Virtually nothing has been written on effective ways of preventing the adopting of self-injurious practices. Indeed, this is an area badly in need of research."[24]

According to the Mayo Clinic, reducing the risk of self-injury will likely include "strategies that involve both individuals and communities— for example, parents, schools, medical professionals, supervisors, co-workers, and coaches."[25] These strategies might include such activities as education and awareness campaigns for schools. One focus could be on encouraging teens to look out for each other; if they suspect a friend is self-injuring and in crisis, they should speak up so the person gets the needed help. Another focus of such campaigns would be educating teens about the power of media influence. "News media, music and other highly visible outlets that feature self-injury may nudge vulnerable children and young adults to experiment," says the Mayo Clinic. "Teaching children critical thinking skills about the influences around them might reduce the harmful impact."[26]

No Easy Answers

Whether they cut, burn, bite, or hit themselves, young people who deliberately self-injure are in trouble. For their own personal reasons they feel unable to cope with unbearable emotions, and they turn to self-injury in a desperate attempt to find relief—a dysfunctional substitute for healthier ways of coping. Teens who admit that they need professional help can and do recover from self-injury if they are treated. If they do not get treatment and continue to harm themselves, they are risking scars and injuries serious enough to last a lifetime.

How Serious a Problem Are Cutting and Self-Injury Among Teens?

66 Self-injury is a behavior that is unfortunately show-ing more frequency in tweens and teenagers. 99

—Jill Emanuele, a child psychologist with the Child Mind Institute.

66 Self-injury is accepted to be especially common in teenagers. 99

—Claire M. Brickell, resident in child and adolescent psychiatry at Boston's Massachusetts General Hospital/ McLean Hospital, and Michael S. Jellinek, professor of psychiatry and pediatrics at Harvard Medical School.

Raychelle Cassada Lohmann is a therapist from South Carolina who specializes in and writes about issues that affect teens, such as self-harm. One day while waiting her turn to be served at a restaurant, Lohmann watched a waitress assist other customers with their orders. "I had seen her there many times," says Lohmann, "but she usually wore long sleeves. Today she had on a tee shirt. I noticed her arms were fully tattooed. I began to study the tattoos and saw that below the vivid tattoos were raised horizontal scars that extended up the inside of her arm. The marks looked like that of a former cutter. The tattoos bore a sad story, of that I was certain. Now at an older age, she had found a way to hide her past." After recognizing the signs of someone who had likely cut herself for years, Lohmann gently asked her about it. "'Yeah, but it's over now,' she said with a reassuring smile."[27]

Lohmann left the restaurant with the waitress's scars weighing heavily on her mind. "She was forever branded by her past," Lohmann writes. "I left the shop thinking 'How can we keep our teens from harming themselves so they don't have to hide their past when they get older? How can we hear their silent cries for help?'"[28] That was when Lohmann decided to start a blog to help educate others about self-harming behaviors.

Difficult to Gauge

Lohmann's reference to "silent cries" is a fitting descriptor for teens who self-injure because they often keep their behavior a secret. They are so ashamed of what they are doing to their bodies that they hide their self-harm from family and friends, sometimes even their closest friends. This secretiveness is a big reason why it is virtually impossible for mental health experts to know exactly how many teens self-harm. Another factor that adds to the uncertainty is that the study of self-injury is a young science; research did not begin until the late 1990s, and no large-scale government studies have been conducted in the United States. American teenagers are regularly surveyed by federal health agencies to evaluate risk-taking behaviors such as sexual activity, smoking, and substance abuse, but the same is not true of self-harm. That is something that researchers hope will change in the not too distant future.

> **The methods used for self-harming differed based on gender, with cutting most common among girls and boys most often hitting themselves.**

One study that focused on self-harm behaviors among youth was conducted by researchers from Denver University in Colorado and Rutgers University in New Jersey. Published in July 2012 in the medical journal *Pediatrics*, the study involved 665 youth between the ages of seven and sixteen. The researchers interviewed the youth to inquire about whether they had engaged in any form of self-injury and found that 53 of them had done so at least once during the past year. This included 7.6 percent of third graders, 4 percent of sixth graders, and 12.7 percent of ninth graders. The methods used for self-harming differed based on gender, with cutting most common among girls and boys most often hitting themselves. "A lot of people tend to think that school-aged children, they're happy, they don't have a lot to worry about," says study author Benjamin L. Hankin from the University of Denver. "Clearly a lot more kids are doing this than people have known."[29]

The Global Picture

Another 2012 study, which focused on the worldwide prevalence of self-injury, was led by University of Wisconsin researcher and noted self-injury expert Jennifer J. Muehlenkamp. The need for such research is explained in the final report, which was published in March 2012 in the journal *Child and Adolescent Psychiatry and Mental Health*. In the report Muehlenkamp and colleagues discuss how existing studies suggest that a significant number of adolescents are likely to engage in self-injury at some point during their lifetimes. "Yet," they add, "there remain a number of inconsistencies within the literature that need to be addressed in order to have a stronger understanding of the true scope of the problem." The authors go on to explain the reasoning behind focusing on worldwide prevalence, even though doing so presented a number of daunting challenges: "The lack of cross-nation comparisons is a striking deficit in the study of self-injury because it precludes drawing conclusions that could inform international policies and efforts to prevent these behaviours among adolescents."[30]

The comprehensive research involved an in-depth examination of fifty-two peer-reviewed, empirical (based on experience rather than only theory) studies of adolescent self-injury that were conducted between January 1, 2005, and December 1, 2011. These studies were published by researchers from the United States, Canada, China, Japan, India, Korea, Australia, New Zealand, and a number of countries in Europe. The focus was limited to lifetime prevalence because many countries that compile data about self-injury do not track six-month or twelve-month prevalence. Muehlenkamp's group made a clear distinction between non-suicidal self-injury (NSSI) and deliberate self-harm (DSH) because, depending on the country, either term may be used. The report states:

The term deliberate self-harm is frequently employed as a more encompassing term for self-injurious behaviours both with and without suicidal intent that have non-fatal outcomes. This term tends to be used predominantly within European countries and in Australia. In contrast, many studies published by researchers within Canada and the United States have employed the term Non-suicidal self-injury (NSSI); the deliberate, self-inflicted destruction of body tissue without suicidal intent and for purposes not socially sanctioned; which explicitly excludes behaviours engaged in with any level of suicidal intention.[31]

After all data from the selected studies were compiled and analyzed, the researchers determined that the worldwide lifetime prevalence of NSSI among adolescents averaged 18 percent. Some of the highest incidence rates were found in Belgium, Germany, and the United States, with Hungary and Japan having the lowest rates. Regarding the evaluation of DSH data, the average lifetime prevalence was found to be 16.1 percent. Norway and the Netherlands had the lowest incidence of DSH, and Italy had the highest.

One especially promising discovery was that worldwide incidence of self-injury among adolescents does not seem to be increasing, which contrasts with suggestions from other researchers and clinicians. The authors write: "Within the past five years the percentage of adolescents reporting NSSI or DSH is relatively consistent and stable. Thus, it appears the global lifetime prevalence of self-injury among community adolescents may have stabilized."[32]

England's Self-Harm Crisis

Although the Muehlenkamp study found that the worldwide prevalence of adolescent self-harm has stabilized, that determination is based on averages; a closer look at certain countries reveals that the problem has been growing. One of these countries is England, where according to a World Health Organization study published in 2014, there has been a threefold increase in the number of teenagers who self-harm. "Our findings are really worrying,"[33] says Fiona Brooks, who was the study's principal investigator for England.

The survey, called *Health Behaviour in School-Aged Children*, has been conducted every four years since 1983. Tens of thousands of youth, aged eleven, thirteen, and fifteen, from more than forty countries are asked questions about their health and well-being, social environments, health-related behaviors, and risk-related behaviors. In all the years the survey was conducted no questions about self-harm were included. England became the first country to include questions about self-harm during the 2013–2014 survey. This was based on reports from teachers in secondary schools throughout England who noticed a significant increase in self-harming behavior among their students. Their concerns were confirmed in the survey, which found that 20 percent of fifteen-year-olds had self-harmed over the past year. This was a significant increase over the 6.9 percent reported during the last comprehensive study, which was published in the *British Medical Journal* in 2002. According to Brooks, the 2013–2014 survey also found that self-harming behavior was much more prevalent among older teenage girls. "Our findings are really worrying," she says, "and it's . . . considerably worse among girls."[34]

> One especially promising discovery was that worldwide incidence of self-injury among adolescents does not seem to be increasing.

One teenager from England who has injured herself since she was twelve years old is a girl named Grace. She used scissors and razor blades and at first cut only her wrists. Then her need to self-harm worsened, and she began cutting all the way up her left arm and the tops of both thighs. "I was hurting myself once a week or even more," says Grace. "Sometimes it was once a month." She explains the short-lived positive effects of cutting. "It calmed me down but then I'd immediately wish I hadn't done it as it hurts and you need to hide it."[35] Although Grace was finally able to stop cutting she still has deep scars from years of doing it. Whenever she is around people she does not know very well, she wears clothing that covers the scars so they are not visible.

Racial Disparity?

In the past many researchers were convinced that self-harm was practiced by Caucasian teens far more often than minority teens. Some research has suggested that this might be true, but most self-injury experts believe that the evidence is inconclusive. Janis Whitlock and Karen Rodham write: "Although a small number of studies comparing Caucasian to non-Caucasian youth show significantly higher rates among the former . . . other studies show similarly high rates in minority samples."[36]

When Washington, DC, writer Janelle Harris learned that her fifteen-year-old daughter had been cutting, she was devastated. "I turned the corner in to her room and my eyes flew to a gash that ran up the middle of her left thigh," she says. "Blood oozed from it; she hovered over it in tears. . . . It wasn't the first time she'd cut. She's been doing it on and off for more than two years. Other parts of her body already bore the scars of her need to release unspoken anxiety and pain." Along with feeling brokenhearted over what her daughter was doing to herself, Harris, who is African American, was also shocked. "Honestly," she says, "it didn't strike me as something black folks do, whatever that means."[37]

> **When Washington, DC, writer Janelle Harris learned that her fifteen-year-old daughter had been cutting, she was devastated.**

In talking with friends and acquaintances Harris found that many of them shared her beliefs about self-harm and race. So she embarked upon a research project and learned that those beliefs were erroneous; cutting and other forms of self-injury were just as prevalent among black teens as white teens. In fact, Harris read a major study from 2010 by British researchers who found that black girls were even more likely to intentionally hurt themselves than white girls. "It's happening to more than just my daughter,"[38] she says.

The study, which was published in the *British Journal of Psychiatry* in September 2010, involved examining thousands of cases of people who visited hospital emergency departments in three cities in England between 2001 and 2006. Of the 20,574 individuals who sought emergency care for injuries related to self-harm, ethnicity data were available for 15,400. The researchers found that in all emergency departments in the three cities, rates of self-harm were highest in young black females aged sixteen to thirty-four. In the city of Manchester, for instance, the rate of self-harm among young black women was 10.3 per 1,000 people, compared with 6.6 per 1,000 people in the white population. "To our knowledge," says lead investigator Jayne Cooper, "this is the first study to show significantly higher rates of self-harm in young black females across a number of cities using large population-based databases."[39] Cooper adds that the results did not provide clear knowledge as to why young black females had higher rates of self-harming behavior.

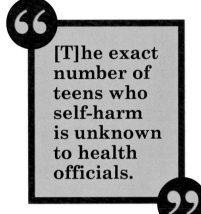

[T]he exact number of teens who self-harm is unknown to health officials.

A Persistent Problem

Although mental health specialists report that self-injury is a formidable problem, the exact number of teens who self-harm is unknown to health officials. Studies have shown, however, that it is a problem not only in the United States but in countries throughout the world. As research continues, and teens who self-injure feel freer to speak openly about it, this may enable health officials to more accurately determine how many young people engage in the practice. Armed with that information, mental health specialists may be in a better position to prevent it.

Primary Source Quotes*

How Serious a Problem Are Cutting and Self-Injury Among Teens?

❝Studies show that far more young people self-harm than their parents realize or will admit to, which is very sad for all concerned.❞

—Jane Smith, *The Parent's Guide to Self-Harm: What Parents Need to Know*. Oxford, UK: Lion, 2012, p. 21.

Smith is director of Anorexia and Bulimia Care, a charity in the United Kingdom that helps teens with eating disorders and those who self-harm.

❝As a psychologist who has been treating teens in San Diego for almost 30 years, I am blown away by recent increases in the numbers of teens who are self harming.❞

—Divya Kakaiya, "Guest Column: Self-Harming Teens Influenced by Social Media," *Pomerado News*, May 16, 2014. www.pomeradonews.com.

Kakaiya is a psychologist, neuroscientist, and school consultant in San Diego, California.

* Editor's Note: While the definition of a primary source can be narrowly or broadly defined, for the purposes of Compact Research, a primary source consists of: 1) results of original research presented by an organization or researcher; 2) eyewitness accounts of events, personal experience, or work experience; 3) first-person editorials offering pundits' opinions; 4) government officials presenting political plans and/or policies; 5) representatives of organizations presenting testimony or policy.

66 **Since many acts of self-harm do not come to the attention of healthcare services, hospital attendance rates do not reflect the true scale of the problem.** 99

—Steven Walker, *Responding to Self-Harm in Children and Adolescents.* London, UK: Jessica Kingsley, 2012, p. 15.

Walker is a psychotherapist from the United Kingdom.

---

66 **Although some teenagers may feel like the steam in the pressure cooker has been released following the act of harming themselves, others may feel hurt, anger, fear and hate.** 99

—American Academy of Child & Adolescent Psychiatry, "Facts for Families: Self-Injury in Adolescents," July 2013. www.aacap.org.

The American Academy of Child & Adolescent Psychiatry represents nearly nine thousand child and adolescent psychiatrists.

---

66 **Many people who self-harm feel that their behaviour is shameful, and such feelings may be reinforced by the stigma that they are unfairly made to feel.** 99

—Neel Burton, "Coping with Self-Harm," *Hide and Seek* (blog), *Psychology Today*, January 13, 2013. www.psychologytoday.com.

Burton is a psychiatrist from Oxford, England.

---

66 **Self-harm, or inflicting physical harm onto one's body to ease emotional distress, is not uncommon in kids and teens.** 99

—Margarita Tartakovsky, "Helping Your Child Reduce Self-Harming Behavior," Psych Central, October 16, 2013. http://psychcentral.com.

Tartakovsky is associate editor for the online mental health resource Psych Central.

66Self-injury can occur in either sex and in any race of people. The behavior is not limited by education, age, sexual orientation, socioeconomic status, or religion.99

—Cleveland Clinic, "Self-Injury," February 4, 2014. http://my.clevelandclinic.org.

Located in Cleveland, Ohio, Cleveland Clinic is an academic medical center that integrates clinical and hospital care with research and education.

66Self-injurious behavior is hard to detect because it is done secretly and on body parts that are relatively easy to hide.99

—Robert T. Muller, "Self-Harm: Know the Signs, Help a Friend," *Talking About Trauma* (blog), *Psychology Today*, June 13, 2014. www.psychologytoday.com.

Muller is a professor of psychology at York University in Toronto, Ontario, Canada.

66The existing data suggest that a significant portion of adolescents are likely to engage in self-injury during their lifetime.99

—Jennifer J. Muehlenkamp et al., "International Prevalence of Adolescent Non-suicidal Self-Injury and Deliberate Self-Harm," *Child and Adolescent Psychiatry and Mental Health*, March 30, 2012. www.capmh.com.

Muehlenkamp is a clinical psychologist and researcher from Eau Claire, Wisconsin.

Facts and Illustrations

How Serious a Problem Are Cutting and Self-Injury Among Teens?

- Mental Health America estimates that **2 million people** in the United States deliberately injure themselves in some way each year, with the majority being teenagers or young adults.

- In a survey released in 2012 of **1,398 British teens**, more than half admitted to self-harming on a daily basis or a few times a week.

- According to Britain's Royal College of Psychiatrists, about **1 in 3 people** who self-harm for the first time will do it again during the following year.

- A 2012 report published in the medical journal *Child and Adolescent Psychiatry and Mental Health* states that the lifetime prevalence of self-injury among adolescents ranges from **12 percent to 23 percent**.

- A 2012 study of **665 youth** published in the medical journal *Pediatrics* found that **12.7 percent** of ninth graders self-injured.

- A 2013 survey of **8,500 students** in Auckland, New Zealand, revealed that **29.1 percent** of girls had self-harmed during the previous year, an increase of over **26 percent** in 2007.

- According to Cornell University researcher Janis Whitlock, research has consistently shown that **6 to 7 percent** of adolescents and young adults engage in self-harming behavior.

2

High Global Prevalence

Health officials throughout the world rarely track self-injury cases, so exact prevalence cannot be determined. From studies that have been conducted, however, researchers can make fairly accurate calculations. One major study published in March 2012 analyzed existing research from a number of countries to determine average worldwide prevalence of self-injurious behavior among adolescents. Different countries use different terms to describe essentially the same behavior, with the two most common terms being non-suicidal self-injury and deliberate self-harm. Due to slight differences in diagnostic criteria, the researchers identified these disorders separately, as reflected in this graph.

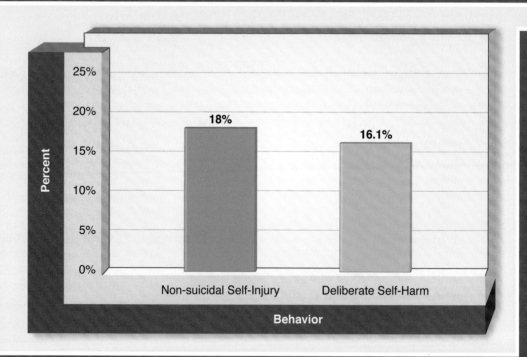

Estimated Worldwide Prevalence of Adolescent Self-Injurious Behavior

Source: Jennifer J. Muehlenkamp et al., "International Prevalence of Adolescent Non-suicidal Self-Injury and Deliberate Self-Harm," *Child and Adolescent Psychiatry and Mental Health*, March 2012. www.capmh.com.

- An April 2013 Boston University article reports that one crisis hotline for young people saw a threefold increase in self-injury–related calls, from **696** in 2007 to **2,052** in 2011.

How Serious a Problem Are Cutting and Self-Injury Among Teens?

Self-Harming Frequency

In August 2014 a team of Swedish researchers published a study that involved 816 adolescents aged fifteen to seventeen. All the teens had self-injured in the past year and when asked how often they did it, nearly 45 percent reported self-injuring eleven times or more.

Past-Year Frequency of Self-Harming Among Teens

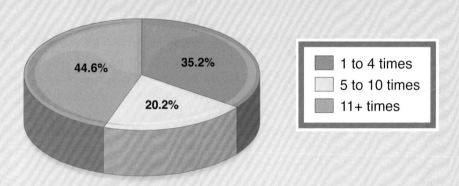

44.6% 35.2% 20.2%

- 1 to 4 times
- 5 to 10 times
- 11+ times

Source: Maria Zetterqvist, "A Cross-Sectional Study of Adolescent Non-Suicidal Self-Injury: Support for a Specific Distress-Function Relationship," *Child and Adolescent Psychiatry and Mental Health*, August 2014. www.capmh.com.

- Self-injury expert Barent Walsh states that in community studies, a range of **6 percent to 25 percent** of youth report self-injuring at least once.

- A 2012 study of **665 youth** published in the medical journal *Pediatrics* found that three times as many adolescent girls engaged in self-injury compared with boys.

- A 2013 survey of **8,500 students** in Auckland, New Zealand, revealed that nearly **18 percent** of boys had self-harmed during the previous year, compared with **15.5 percent** in 2007.

- According to Cornell University researcher Janis Whitlock, studies have shown that among teens who self-injure, **20 to 25 percent** report more than **10 lifetime incidents**.

Self-Injury Prevalence Varies by Gender

Males and females of all ages have engaged in self-harming, but some research shows that it is more prevalent among adolescent females. For example, a study published in July 2012 found that for children in third and sixth grades, self-harm was more common among boys; but by the ninth grade, girls were nearly four times as likely as boys to self-injure.

Rates of Self-Injury by Grade and Gender

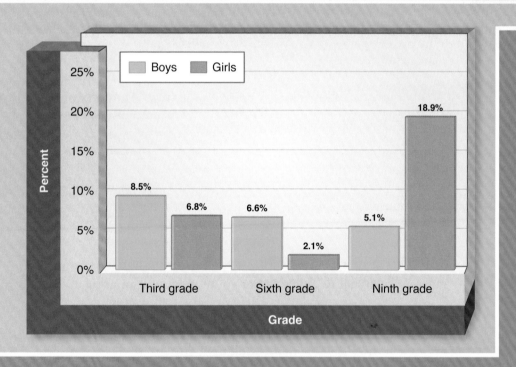

Source: Andrea L. Barrocas et al., "Rates of Nonsuicidal Self-Injury in Youth: Age, Sex, and Behavioral Methods in a Community Sample," *Pediatrics*, July 2012. www.ncbi.nlm.nih.gov.

- A survey released in 2012 of **1,398 British teens** revealed that boys were significantly less likely to tell anyone about their self-harming than girls.

What Causes Teens to Deliberately Harm Themselves?

> **"**Like substance abuse, adolescent self-harming behavior has no one single cause. It cuts across all cultural and socioeconomic levels.**"**
>
> —American Association for Marriage and Family Therapy, the professional association for marriage and family therapists.

> **"**Research has shown that many people who harm themselves are struggling with intolerable distress or unbearable situations. A person will often struggle with difficulties for some time before they self-harm.**"**
>
> —Royal College of Psychiatrists, the United Kingdom's professional organization responsible for education, training, and setting and raising standards in psychiatry.

Today, scientists are able to pinpoint the causes of numerous human diseases and disorders, but psychiatric conditions are much more challenging to understand. This is true of self-injury: Even though research has provided many clues about the underlying reasons young people deliberately hurt themselves, no one can say with any certainty what actually causes this behavior. One factor mental health specialists widely agree on is that most who self-injure are feeling overwhelmed by emotional pain and are desperate for some outlet to release it. So they cut themselves or self-injure in other ways. This is not a healthy way of coping with problems, and self-harming teens usually know that, which is why they feel regret and shame afterward. But for those who are deeply troubled, self-injuring might seem like their only option. "In other words," say psychiatrists Claire M. Brickell and Michael S. Jellinek, "the *problem* for the patient is feeling unbearably sad, anxious, or lonely—or not feeling anything at all. Self-injury is a *solution* that, in the short term, can be incredibly effective at easing intolerable emotions."[40]

Stressed-Out Teens

When asked by a therapist why they self-injure, many teens cite stress that seems overwhelming at times. This is more common among today's youth than people often realize. For instance, a February 2014 report by the American Psychological Association shows that teens are far more stressed than was previously known: Twenty-seven percent admitted to being extremely stressed during the past school year. In fact, some mental health professionals say that today's teens are under more pressure and have more stress than teens have in the past. "The truth is that teens face an enormous amount of life stressors and pressure," says Raychelle Cassada Lohmann. "From academics to their social life, many teens are consumed with many difficult life transitions. And yes, to top it off they're going through puberty. Adolescence isn't an easy time for teens or their parents. It is important for teens to have safe outlets to express their feelings and concerns."[41]

> "One factor mental health specialists widely agree on is that most who self-injure are feeling overwhelmed by emotional pain and are desperate for some outlet to release it."

According to fourteen-year-old Carly (not her real name), nothing in life is more stressful than change. Between 2013, when she had to switch to a different middle school, and the next year, when she was trying to get into a private high school, it felt as though her whole world was changing before her eyes. So, she started cutting herself. "Everything became so overwhelming that it pushed me over the edge," says Carly. Before long the stress got so unbearable that she was cutting herself every day. "I was sick of feeling that pain and stress in my head," she says. "When I felt physical pain, it took that away. I know it wasn't a good thing, but I thought the stress I was feeling was worse."[42]

A young lesbian woman named Alicia (not Alicia Moore) began cutting herself when she was a high school freshman. She had talked with her family about her sexual orientation, and they refused to accept it. Alicia found this to be extraordinarily painful and an immense source of stress. She says she used to cut herself whenever she was angry, upset, or stressed out. "Self-harm was a way for me to forget about everything," she explains. "I had no way to deal with emotional pain." Like many who self-injure, Alicia felt relief immediately after cutting herself, but it was quickly followed by regret. "I hate feeling this crazy all the time," she says. "It's a struggle."[43]

The Scourge of Bullying

Bullying has always been an unfortunate factor in the lives of children, but that does not mean it should be taken lightly or dismissed as just part of growing up. Many children who are bullied over a long period of time suffer emotionally because of it, questioning their self-worth and feeling lonely and insecure. Researchers have learned that bullying can cause children to be severely stressed—and it can also lead them to start harming themselves later in life. According to a report published in the June 2013 issue of the journal *Child & Adolescent Psychiatry*, when young children are bullied, this vastly increases their chance of self-harming during their teenage years. A team of British researchers followed nearly five thousand children from South West England who participated in a major United Kingdom study called *Children of the 90s*, referring to young adults who were born between April 1991 and December 1992.

The study participants were assessed for exposure to bullying when they were between the ages of eight and ten. Those who were identified as having been bullied were asked whether they had engaged in self-harm when they were sixteen or seventeen. The researchers learned that those who had been victims of chronic bullying as children were nearly five times more likely to self-harm as teens than children who had not been bullied. University of Warwick professor Dieter Wolke, one of the researchers involved in the study, explains the significance of this finding: "It is further evidence for doing away with the myth that bullying at a young age can be viewed as a harmless rite of passage." Wolke says he would like to see physicians routinely questioning children about bullying because "many children suffer in silence and never speak out about being bullied." He continues: "The importance of this early intervention should not be understated. If we were able to eliminate bullying, while other exposures remained constant, there would be a potential to prevent 20 percent of all self-harm cases."[44]

Lingering emotional pain from being bullied was the catalyst for Shavontaye Logwood to begin cutting when she was thirteen. She had been relentlessly bullied in the fifth and sixth grades and even though it had stopped, her memories of that painful time were as vivid as ever. Kids had teased her about her appearance, making comments about her weight, her hair, and her clothes. "I hadn't gotten over it completely," she says of the night she finally broke. She was sitting in her bedroom crying and felt as though she could not take any more pain. "I kept thinking about the cruel names I was called," she says, "all of the pointing and laughing, all of the random hurtful comments directed towards me. I thought about how sad I felt on a daily basis and how angry I was at the whole world for no real reason at all." Thinking that physical pain might diminish her emotional pain, Logwood grabbed a pencil sharpener, broke it, and pulled out the razor blade. She wiped the blade with an alcohol pad and sliced open her skin—and then sat there watching herself bleed. "It hurt so badly and I regretted it as soon as I did it," she says, "but at the same time, I felt like it was the only way out."[45]

> "Researchers have learned that bullying can cause children to be severely stressed—and it can also lead them to start harming themselves later in life."

That experience was just the beginning of Logwood's self-harming. For the next two years she cut herself on a regular basis and also hurt herself in other ways such as hitting, pinching, scratching, and biting. "I was a mess," she says, "and I thought that I would never be able to stop my self-abusive behavior. And actually, I didn't even want to. At one point, things got so bad that I started to do it just for fun; the pain actually felt good."[46]

A Puzzling and Disturbing Trend

Although no two teens who self-injure are exactly the same, the one commonality they share is that some kind of psychological trauma lies at the root of their behavior. In recent years, however, psychologists and school counselors throughout the United States have seen growth in the number of teens who are cutting themselves and do not fit the profile of teens who are self-harming due to emotional pain. "They want to do it because other kids are doing it, period," says San Diego, California, clinical psychologist Divya Kakaiya, who has been in practice for thirty years. "These are not high-risk kids," she says. "It's become a way of belongingness in middle school, to be part of the popular group."[47]

Kakaiya, who refers to this problem as an epidemic, says that teens sometimes cut themselves as a group activity, perhaps sharing cutting instruments. Unlike the secretive behavior that has long been typical of self-injurers, these girls show off their scars by wearing shorts and shirts with short sleeves. Because of the sense of urgency surrounding this trend, Kakaiya has been asked to speak about it at middle schools. "I was at a middle school a month ago where there were three large groups of girls," she says, adding that each group had about twelve students. "All of them were self-harming in school and teaching [others] the best ways to cut."[48] Kakaiya and others who work with young people say that smartphones are perpetuating the problem. Teens take pictures of their cutting wounds and share them on Instagram, Tumblr, Snapchat, and Twitter, which can serve as a trigger for other vulnerable young people.

> " Teens take pictures of their cutting wounds and share them on Instagram, Tumblr, Snapchat, and Twitter, which can serve as a trigger for other vulnerable young people. "

Online Promotion of Self-Harm

As indispensable as the Internet is for everything from communication to shopping, checking bank balances, and socializing with friends, it is also a vehicle for dangerous activities. In recent years health officials and mental health specialists have become alarmed at the proliferation of websites and online forums that encourage young people to self-injure. These sites appear to be against self-harm behaviors, but many are intentionally misrepresenting their true purpose.

"The epidemic of self-harm is completely being transmitted virally via social media and the Internet," says Kakaiya. "There are hundreds of blogs on the Internet that glorify self-harm. Middle school girls feel an enhanced sense of belongingness when they are part of 'the' club that cuts."[49]

One young man, who appears in a video on the mental health site Healthy Place, used to visit and participate in pro–self-injury websites when he was sixteen or seventeen. At the time he was self-harming on a regular basis. He says people he interacted with on the sites provided him with ideas for how to self-injure and how to better hide his wounds and scars. "I really wish I hadn't found those sites," he says, "because it just made it harder to stop [self-injuring]. They'd be like, 'Oh, do this' and I was like, 'Oh, that's a really good idea,' then I'd ask how to hide it and they'd tell me. It's a really bad community. These people say they really care about you but really they're just helping you kill yourself."[50]

> "Of fifteen teenagers who had harmed themselves in violent ways, 80 percent said they had gone online to research self-injury beforehand."

A study conducted in 2013 by researchers from England's University of Oxford found a strong link between heavy Internet use and self-injury. Of fifteen teenagers who had harmed themselves in violent ways, 80 percent said they had gone online to research self-injury beforehand. Of thirty-four teens who had self-harmed by cutting, 73 percent said they had researched it online. Says lead study author Kate Daine, a postgraduate researcher from the Centre for Evidence-Based Intervention: "There are no known online interventions to date that specifically target young people at risk of self-harm or suicide and yet we find that adolescents who self-harm are very frequent users of the internet. While social media might be useful for supporting vulnerable adolescents, we also find that the internet is doing more harm than good in some cases. We need to know more about how we can use social media as a channel to help young people in distress."[51]

A Complex Combination of Causes

When young people intentionally harm themselves, there are no simple answers to why they do it. In general, the need to self-harm arises because of severe emotional pain, and the causes of that pain differ from person to person. Contributing factors include high levels of stress, unhappy family environment, being bullied as a child, and Internet influence. In some cases, teens may self-harm simply because their peers are doing it, although that is not considered typical self-injurious behavior. As more is learned about self-injury, researchers will undoubtedly know more about underlying causes.

Primary Source Quotes*

What Causes Teens to Deliberately Harm Themselves?

❝Many children who self-harm struggle with internal conflicts, usually experiencing depression, anxiety, or other serious psychological concerns.❞

—Deborah Serani, *Depression and Your Child: A Guide for Parents and Caregivers*. Lanham, MD: Rowman & Littlefield, 2013, p. 84.

Serani is a clinical psychologist and author whose specialty is depression.

❝There are young people who self-harm who have a nasty history of emotional, physical and sexual abuse.❞

—Steven Walker, *Responding to Self-Harm in Children and Adolescents*. London, UK: Jessica Kingsley, 2012, p. 11.

Walker is a psychotherapist from the United Kingdom.

* Editor's Note: While the definition of a primary source can be narrowly or broadly defined, for the purposes of Compact Research, a primary source consists of: 1) results of original research presented by an organization or researcher; 2) eyewitness accounts of events, personal experience, or work experience; 3) first-person editorials offering pundits' opinions; 4) government officials presenting political plans and/or policies; 5) representatives of organizations presenting testimony or policy.

> **If we look more closely at what adolescence is and how it affects those going through it, then we can learn to understand why self-harming behaviour largely occurs in the adolescent years.**

—Jane Smith, *The Parent's Guide to Self-Harm: What Parents Need to Know.* Oxford, UK: Lion, 2012, p. 36.

Smith is director of Anorexia and Bulimia Care, a charity in the United Kingdom that helps teens with eating disorders and those who self-harm.

> **People who have friends who intentionally harm themselves are more likely to begin self-injuring.**

—Mayo Clinic, "Self-Injury/Cutting," December 6, 2012. www.mayoclinic.org.

Mayo Clinic is a world-renowned health care facility headquartered in Rochester, Minnesota.

> **Adolescents who have difficulty talking about their feelings may show their emotional tension, physical discomfort, pain and low self-esteem with self-injurious behaviors.**

—American Academy of Child & Adolescent Psychiatry, "Facts for Families: Self-Injury in Adolescents," July 2013. www.aacap.org.

The American Academy of Child & Adolescent Psychiatry represents nearly nine thousand child and adolescent psychiatrists.

> **Teenagers turn to self-injury as a solution to problems for various reasons, including genetics, temperament, or particular stressors.**

—Claire M. Brickell and Michael S. Jellinek, "Self-Injury: Why Teens Do It, How to Help," *Contemporary Pediatrics*, March 1, 2014. http://contemporarypediatrics.modernmedicine.com.

Brickell is a resident in child and adolescent psychiatry at Boston's Massachusetts General Hospital/McLean Hospital, and Jellinek is professor of psychiatry and pediatrics at Harvard Medical School.

❝Usually when people harm themselves, they are suffering a great deal inside.❞

—Women's and Children's Health Network, "Self-Harm," Teen Health, March 5, 2014. www.cyh.com.

The Women's and Children's Health Network promotes health, well-being, and development of children, young people, and families throughout South Australia.

❝Girls who self-cut often have lifestyles that are too stressful or lifestyles that lack healthy balance.❞

—Lucie Hemmen, "Teen Girls: A Crash Course: Stressed Out Teen Girls: Cutting to Cope," *Psychology Today*, November 28, 2012. www.psychologytoday.com.

Hemmen is a clinical psychologist with a private practice in Santa Cruz, California.

Facts and Illustrations

What Causes Teens to Deliberately Harm Themselves?

- In a 2012 survey of **1,398 British teens**, feeling depressed was the main reason participants gave for hurting themselves.

- A June 2012 report by Italian researchers states that **40 percent to 80 percent** of adolescents with diagnosed psychiatric conditions (such as borderline personality disorder) have engaged in self-harm.

- University of Missouri Medical Center psychiatrist Armando R. Favazza says that half the people who self-harm report a history of childhood sexual abuse.

- According to the Mayo Clinic, evidence suggests that self-injury is more common among people who have a family history of self-injury, suicide, or self-destructive acts.

- A study published in December 2012 by Swedish researchers found that **20 percent** of teens who lost a parent to cancer had self-injured compared with **10 percent** of teens who had not experienced that kind of trauma.

- According to Cornell University researcher Janis Whitlock, youth identifying as bisexual or questioning their sexuality have been shown to be at significantly elevated risk for self-injury compared to both their heterosexual and homosexual peers.

Risk Factors for Self-Injury

Mental health experts say that there is no one cause for self-harming behavior; rather, it can develop due to a number of factors, such as those shown here.

Potential Causes of Self-Harming Behavior	
Factor	**Behavior**
Age	Self-harming often starts during early adolescence when emotions are more volatile and teens face increasing pressures and conflict.
Personality traits	Those who self-injure are more likely to be impulsive, explosive, highly self-critical, and poor problem-solvers.
Gender	Females are at greater risk of self-harming than males.
Having friends who self-injure	Those with friends who intentionally harm themselves are more likely to begin self-injuring.
Excessive alcohol or drug use	Many people who self-harm do so while under the influence of alcohol or drugs.
Childhood trauma	Some people who self-injure were neglected; sexually, physically, or emotionally abused; or experienced other traumatic events during childhood.
Life issues	Many people who self-injure grew up (and still remain) in an unstable family environment; and/or they may question their personal identity or sexuality.
Mental health issues	Self-injury has been linked to mental disorders such as borderline personality disorder, depression, anxiety disorders, post-traumatic stress disorder, and eating disorders.

Source: Mayo Clinic, "Self-Injury/Cutting," December 6, 2012. www.mayoclinic.org.

Self-Harm Is Linked to Childhood Distress

In August 2014 a team of Swedish researchers published a study of 816 adolescents who had self-harmed at some point during the previous year. One finding in the study was that a high percentage of the youth had experienced some form of abuse, trauma, or other types of adversity.

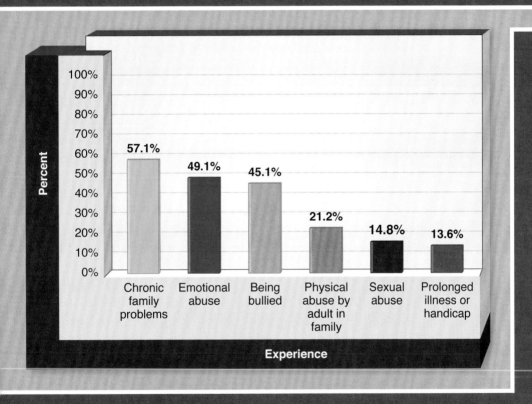

Percentage of Self-Harming Youth Who Have Experienced . . .

Source: Maria Zetterqvist et al., "A Cross-Sectional Study of Adolescent Non-Suicidal Self-Injury: Support for a Specific Distress-Function Relationship," *Child and Adolescent Psychiatry and Mental Health*, August 2014. www.capmh.com.

- A study published in September 2012 by Italian researchers found that adolescent self-injurers had poorer relationships with their mothers and more sexual and physical abuse episodes than non-injurers.

British Teens Reveal Why They First Self-Harmed

A poll completed in 2014 and conducted by four health charities in the United Kingdom asked 1,398 teens to share information about their self-harming behaviors, including why they chose to self-harm and how they felt at the time. The most common responses are shown here.

Main Reasons Teens Gave for Hurting Themselves the First Time

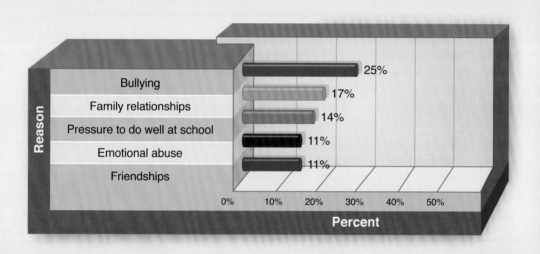

Most Common Feelings That Led to Teens Hurting Themselves

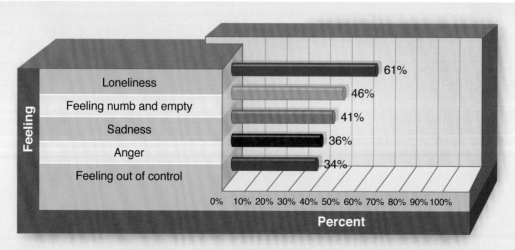

Source: Emma Motherwell, "Self-Harm: Youth Charities Reveal Bullying and Loneliness as a Major Trigger," YouthNet, February 27, 2014. www.youthnet.org.

- The Mayo Clinic states that teens who self-injure are those who have a hard time regulating, expressing, or understanding emotions.

- According to Cornell University researcher Janis Whitlock, the adolescent stage of life is in itself a risk factor for self-injury.

- A 2014 study of German teens revealed that those with alternative lifestyles (such as Goth) were **3 to 4 times** more likely to self-injure than other teens.

- According to the Mayo Clinic, excessive alcohol or drug use increases the risk of self-injury among teens.

- Cornell University researcher Janis Whitlock states that the Internet plays an important role in the growth of self-injury because it serves as a platform for hundreds of self-harm–related message boards, YouTube videos, and social networking sites.

What Are the Risks of Cutting and Self-Injury?

❝Self-injurious behavior can cause irreparable physical damage and can even lead to death, from cutting too deeply, getting an infection or going into shock.❞

—Harrell Woodson, a psychologist with the Menninger Clinic in Houston, Texas.

❝I feel so emotional about this because I really really want to help everyone avoid self-injury. It is such a trap, it ruins everything.❞

—Erin, a young woman who has self-injured by cutting since she was fifteen years old.

P hysicians and other health care practitioners emphasize that young people who deliberately harm themselves are opening the door to numerous problems, some of which can be severe and life-threatening. Those who self-harm by cutting, for instance, risk infection because bacteria and other organisms can easily get into open wounds. Infection is even more likely among people who share cutting implements—and even more serious is the potential for contracting the liver disease hepatitis or HIV. Newtown Square, Pennsylvania, physician Mary L. Gavin explains: "It is possible to get the human immunodeficiency virus (HIV, the virus that leads to AIDS) from sharing cutting instruments—such as a needle or knife—that might have the virus on them. The virus that causes hepatitis also can be spread through cutting."[52]

Teens who self-harm by burning can cause sores that become infected, and having this sort of infection treated can be very painful. Those who use chemicals or acids to burn themselves are taking an elevated risk, as Hamish Laing explains: "These can cause massive destruction and people can even lose limbs. Potentially it can be life threatening."[53] Another deadly possibility is severe blood loss if someone who is cutting accidentally cuts into a major blood vessel or artery.

Scarred by Scars

Most everyone who self-injures by cutting or carving into their flesh will have to live with scars for the rest of their lives. According to Laing, this can come as a surprise to people who assume that they can have scars surgically removed later. Often, he says, very little can be done to minimize heavy scarring. He explains: "It's important to remember that all injuries will leave permanent scarring. . . . It's important to get help so that wounds won't become infected, as that always makes scarring worse."[54]

A young woman named Erin, who started cutting when she was fifteen, now has more than two hundred scars on various parts of her body. On her blog *Daisies and Bruises* she talks candidly about the damage she has done to her body from years of cutting herself. For a long time Erin hid her scars but she no longer makes the effort. "I stopped hiding my scars about four or five years ago," she says. Even though this was a conscious decision, Erin says it causes her embarrassment because she must endure a lot of staring. "People with scars from accidents undoubtedly receive a lot of stares," she says, "but when you've scarred yourself, there is extra stigma involved." She writes:

> "Teens who self-harm by burning can cause sores that become infected, and having this sort of infection treated can be very painful.

In the summer, a lot of strangers see my scars and sometimes I'm having a fairly good day until I see someone staring at my arms. Sometimes they ask me what happened, other times they look at me like I'm possessed.

When I'm having a good day, I can't see my body without being reminded of all my bad days. I want to grow as a person and change, and my scars remind me of my painful past every time I see them. Last weekend I was out shopping and two girls who looked to be about eleven stared at me, completely dumbfounded. They looked horrified and terrified and I just felt so awful.[55]

From Casual Cutting to Hopeless Addiction

In the same way that teens can become hooked on drugs, tobacco, and alcohol, self-harming behavior can also become an addiction. According to Janis Whitlock, this is because the burst of relief that someone feels after cutting is actually endorphins being released in the brain, a process, Whitlock says, "that increases the possibility of becoming addicted to self-injury."[56] This can lead to a vicious cycle: A teen self-harms, gets momentary relief, and unconsciously learns to associate this relief with the pain of self-harm. Once the pain of self-harming fades the emotional tension returns, and the teen feels the need to self-harm again. Unless measures are taken to break this destructive cycle, it can continue indefinitely.

> In the same way that teens can become hooked on drugs, tobacco, and alcohol, self-harming behavior can also become an addiction.

Erin warns young people who are curious about cutting that the practice can be addicting—and can quickly spiral out of control. She says it is easy to convince oneself that the cutting will stop after a bit of scratching, but self-harm does not stop there—it accelerates and becomes more risky and potentially life-threatening as the cutting continues. "What do I mean by 'accelerating?'" Erin asks. "I mean that I started by scratching myself a teeny tiny bit, injuries that initially didn't leave scars. Over time, each injury became slightly worse, slightly deeper to the point of threatening my life. I am honestly very *very* lucky that I haven't bled to death by accident, or gotten an infection that killed me. I could have injured muscles or tendons and lost feeling and movement in my hands."[57]

A teenage girl named Kris admits having an addiction to cutting, and her self-harming behavior accelerated in the way Erin describes. At first Kris was cutting herself about once a week, but before long it grew to two to three times a week. Then it was once a day, and eventually she was cutting four to five times a day. "I stopped eating lunch in the cafeteria and started locking myself in the bathroom and cutting while I ate," she says. "Now that's an addiction to cutting! A few times, the blood seeped through to my jeans and if anyone asked, I always told them that I spilled ketchup or chocolate on me at lunch."[58]

> **Some people who find self-harm to be especially soothing become so dependent on it that they cannot imagine living without it.**

Today Kris has hundreds of scars on her body, with most on her upper thighs. She says the most frustrating thing is that she does not see an end to it; she has no idea how she will ever stop self-injuring. "I don't know how to make this better," she says. "I mean it's me. You think that I could just say I'm not going to cut anymore. Yet somehow it's much harder than that. You have to want to stop. And even though I know that I should, that doesn't mean I do. . . . In fact, stopping is probably the hardest thing I've ever done. Like I said, I'm not just a teenager cutting myself. I think I'm a cutter with a cutting addiction."[59]

Dangerous Obsession

Some people who find self-harm to be especially soothing become so dependent on it that they cannot imagine living without it. It becomes not just their main way of coping but their only way of coping. They become obsessed with hurting themselves, and theirs is a condition that is both extreme and dangerous. This was the case with a British woman named Claire Shorthand, who began self-harming when she was fourteen. "My feelings would build up like a volcano," she says, "and hurting myself gave me a release and allowed me to disconnect from life for a while."[60]

At the worst point of her illness, Shorthand was self-harming at least ten times each day and was hospitalized three or four times a week. She cut herself with scissors and razor blades and burned herself with cigarettes, leaving a criss-cross of scars and wounds up and down her legs and arms. Once she even inserted scissors in her leg and left them there for days. The turning point came when Shorthand inserted nine ball-point pens in her leg and nearly had to have her leg amputated. She had the pens surgically removed except for one that was pushed too deep in the tissue of her leg. Surgeons could not safely remove it and the pen remains in her leg today. "If I hadn't had help," says Shorthand, "I would have been dead by the time I was 20."[61]

A Gateway to Suicide

Mental health specialists emphasize that teens who cut themselves or self-harm in other ways are generally not interested in ending their lives. Rather, they are trying to cope with unbearable emotions and turn to self-harm rather than choosing healthier methods of coping. But this is one of the ironic aspects of self-injury: Even though the nature of it is not suicidal, and its official name is listed in the DSM as *non-suicidal self-injury*, those who regularly engage in the practice have a markedly higher suicide risk than those who do not. Whitlock explains: "While we can't conclude that self-injury leads to later suicide attempts, it is a red flag that someone is distressed and at greater risk. This is important because self-injury is a relatively new behavior that does not show up much in the literature as a risk factor for suicide. It also suggests that if someone with self-injury history becomes suicidal, having engaged in NSSI may make it much easier to carry out the physical actions needed to lethally damage the body."[62]

Analyzing this trend was the focus of a study conducted in 2012 by Whitlock and her colleagues. Participants, mostly in their early twenties, answered a confidential mental health survey annually for three years. The survey assessed their history of self-harming behaviors and suicidal thoughts and behaviors, along with gathering demographic information and common protective and risk factors. Whitlock's team found that, independent of other risk factors, young people who had self-injured were nearly three times as likely to attempt suicide or have suicidal thoughts. At even greater risk were those with a history of five or more instances of self-injury, who were found to be four times more likely to attempt suicide or have suicidal thoughts. Given the prevalence of self-injury, Whitlock encourages physicians and others who work with young people to be better trained to spot such behaviors and assess for suicide risk.

The study identified two factors that appear to help lower the suicide risk in young people with a history of self-harming behavior. Participants who had confided in their parents about their distress, and those who saw reasons for living, were significantly less likely to show suicidal thoughts and behaviors. "Meaning in life as a protective factor is not so surprising, because many who attempt suicide report that they feel a deep and often chronic lack of life meaning," says Whitlock. "However, considering that we studied a college population, it's a surprise that the parents emerged as having such a powerful influence in young adults' mental well-being, especially since we looked at respondents' relationships with all kinds of people, including therapists. Treatments for people at risk for suicide should focus on strengthening these relationships when feasible."[63]

One especially tragic case of a troubled, self-harming teen committing suicide occurred in London, England, in January 2014. Fifteen-year-old Tallulah Wilson, a pretty and talented ballet dancer, was killed when hit by a train. An inquest followed her death and determined that she had intentionally thrown herself in front of the train as it sped down the tracks. The teen suffered from depression and had been injuring herself for a long time. A few days before her death Wilson's mother found that her daughter had been active on Tumblr and had thousands of followers. "She was in the clutches of a toxic digital world where in the final few weeks we could no longer reach her,"[64] says the girl's mother.

On the Tumblr site Wilson had posted about drinking alcohol and taking cocaine and also uploaded graphic pictures of herself in the midst of self-injury. "It was pictures of her cutting herself," her mother said during the inquest. "It's like the worst horror movie you have ever seen in your house." On the site, her mother saw other disturbing images. "I realised there were young girls on there cutting themselves to see who is worse."[65]

> "This is one of the ironic aspects of self-injury: Even though the nature of it is not suicidal . . . those who regularly engage in the practice have a markedly higher suicide risk than those who do not.

Prolific Risks

From permanent scarring to infections and life-threatening blood loss, the dangers associated with self-injury are many and varied. Teens may think that they can limit their cutting, burning, or other self-harming methods to only minor injuries, and some are able to do that. But there is also the risk of becoming so obsessed with self-harming that it seems impossible and unbearable to live without it.

Primary Source Quotes*

What Are the Risks of Cutting and Self-Injury?

"The severity of the act can vary from superficial wounds to those resulting in lasting disfigurement."

—Cornell University Research Program on Self-Injury and Recovery, "What Is Self-Injury?" 2013. www.selfinjury.bctr.cornell.edu.

The Cornell Research Program on Self-Injury and Recovery conducts research to help teens and adults who self-injure, along with their friends and families.

"Even though fads come and go, most of the wounds on the adolescents' skin will be permanent."

—American Academy of Child & Adolescent Psychiatry, "Facts for Families: Self-Injury in Adolescents," July 2013. www.aacap.org.

The American Academy of Child & Adolescent Psychiatry represents nearly nine thousand child and adolescent psychiatrists.

* Editor's Note: While the definition of a primary source can be narrowly or broadly defined, for the purposes of Compact Research, a primary source consists of: 1) results of original research presented by an organization or researcher; 2) eyewitness accounts of events, personal experience, or work experience; 3) first-person editorials offering pundits' opinions; 4) government officials presenting political plans and/or policies; 5) representatives of organizations presenting testimony or policy.

"People who self-injure sometimes hurt themselves repeatedly, and often have scars."

—Center for Young Women's Health, "Self-Injury," February 27, 2014. www.youngwomenshealth.org.

The Center for Young Women's Health, which is part of Boston Children's Hospital, helps educate teenage girls on normal health and development as well as diseases and disorders.

"Deep cutting may indicate that the young person dissociates during the act of self-harm; even if the intent is not suicide, this kind of cutting is extremely dangerous and can lead to permanent tissue damage or death."

—InnerChange, "Cutting and Self-Harm," 2013. www.innerchange.com.

InnerChange is a residential treatment facility located in Orem, Utah.

"The most concerning fact that research shows is that deliberate, nonsuicidal self-injury can lead to deliberate suicide."

—Deborah Serani, *Depression and Your Child: A Guide for Parents and Caregivers*. Lanham, MD: Rowman & Littlefield, 2013, p. 84.

Serani is a clinical psychologist and author whose specialty is depression.

"Self-harming behavior can be dangerous, particularly if the youth is abusing alcohol and other drugs."

—American Association for Marriage and Family Therapy, "Adolescent Self-Harm," 2013. www.aamft.org.

The American Association for Marriage and Family Therapy is the professional association for marriage and family therapists.

❝It is possible that a cut might be deeper than intended by the cutter. The result could be deadly or severely damaging depending on the placement of the cut.❞

—Anne Lawton, "The Truth About Self-Harm and Cutting," Pathways Professional Counseling, August 8, 2013. www.pathwaysprofessional.org.

Lawton is a therapist with Pathways Professional Counseling in Birmingham, Alabama.

....

❝Cutting can give you permanent scarring. If nerves or tendons are damaged by cutting, this can lead to numbness or weakness.❞

—Royal College of Psychiatrists, "Self-Harm," July 2014. www.rcpsych.ac.uk.

The Royal College of Psychiatrists is the United Kingdom's professional organization responsible for education, training, and setting and raising standards in psychiatry.

....

Facts and Illustrations

What Are the Risks of Cutting and Self-Injury?

- Clinical psychologist Wendy Lader states that people who self-injure are **9 times** more likely to attempt suicide than non–self-injurers.

- According to Britain's Royal College of Psychiatrists, about **3 in 100 people** who self-harm over a long period of time will commit suicide, which is significantly higher than the rate for those who do not self-harm.

- A 2013 publication by researchers from the University of Oxford in England states that between **40 percent and 60 percent** of people who die by suicide have a history of at least one episode of deliberate self-harm.

- According to the Mayo Clinic, one of the most significant risks of cutting is life-threatening problems, such as blood loss if major blood vessels or arteries are cut.

- The New York Department of Health states that self-inflicted injuries are the second leading cause of hospitalizations due to injury for teens **aged 15 to 19**.

- According to researchers Patrick L. Kerr, Jennifer J. Muehlenkamp, and James M. Turner, among self-injurers who commit suicide, cutting accounts for only about **1.4 percent to 2 percent** of the deaths.

Self-Harm Can Be Hazardous to Health

Teens who deliberately harm themselves are risking complications ranging from minor (such as light bleeding from small cuts and scratches) to serious enough to be life-threatening (severe blood loss and/or infections). Shown here are some of the problems that can develop as a result of self-injury.

Problems Caused by Self-Injury
Psychological distress such as worsening feelings of shame, guilt, and other painful emotions.
Infection from wounds or from sharing cutting implements.
Accidental severe injury such as life-threatening blood loss or infection.
Permanent scars and/or disfigurement from healed injuries.
Increased risk for suicide.

Source: University of Massachusetts Medical School, "Self-Injury." www.umassmed.edu.

- In a 2012 study of **665 youth** published in the medical journal *Pediatrics,* **25 percent** of boys and **15 percent** of girls self-harmed in ways deemed as "other," one of which was throwing their bodies into sharp objects.

- According to a July 2014 fact sheet from the Centers for Disease Control and Prevention, in a given year an estimated **713,000 people** visit hospital emergency rooms because of self-inflicted injuries.

- Mental health experts say that one of the most significant risks for teens who self-harm by head banging is long-term damage to the brain.

Putting Health at Risk

Medical providers emphasize that young people who deliberately injure themselves are taking a risk—a life-threatening risk, in some cases, such as blood loss from deep cutting, severe infection from cutting or burning, or concussion from banging the head on hard surfaces. During a 2014 poll, respondents were asked how they regularly injured themselves and their answers revealed an alarming variety of self-harming methods. Shown here are the results of the poll.

What Methods of Self-Injury Do You Regularly Use?

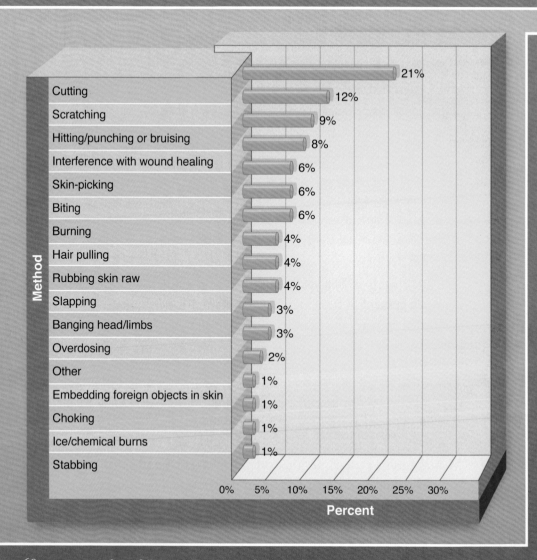

Method	Percent
Cutting	21%
Scratching	12%
Hitting/punching or bruising	9%
Interference with wound healing	8%
Skin-picking	6%
Biting	6%
Burning	6%
Hair pulling	4%
Rubbing skin raw	4%
Slapping	4%
Banging head/limbs	3%
Overdosing	3%
Other	2%
Embedding foreign objects in skin	1%
Choking	1%
Ice/chemical burns	1%
Stabbing	1%

Source: Self-Injury.net, "What Methods of Self-Injury Do You Regularly Use?" March 28, 2014. http://self-injury.net.

- A December 2012 study led by Cornell University researcher Janis Whitlock found self-injury to precede or coincide with suicidal thoughts and/or behaviors in more than **60 percent** of cases.

- According to Options Behavioral Health, it is not unusual for substance abuse disorders to develop as self-injuring teens attempt to ease stress by self-medicating, which then elevates the risk of further self-harming.

- The New York Department of Health reports that each year in New York State, more than **2,300 teens** aged fifteen to nineteen are seen in hospital emergency departments for self-inflicted injuries.

Can Teens Overcome the Need to Self-Injure?

> 66Stopping self-injury can be like quitting drugs or alcohol. It's challenging, but with support, resources, and a good plan, you can do it!99

> —Center for Young Women's Health, which helps educate teenage girls on normal health and development as well as diseases and disorders.

> 66Treating self-injury behavior can take time, hard work and your own desire to recover.99

> —Mayo Clinic, a world-renowned health care facility headquartered in Rochester, Minnesota.

For Alicia Moore to stop cutting herself was a monumental task. It had been her only way of coping with severe emotional pain since she was in the fifth grade. As an excellent student and talented musician and dancer, she stood out among her peers—but not in a way that made her happy. "I'd get made fun of for being smart," she says. "Getting A's on tests. Stuff like that. It was devastating. I thought there was something wrong with me. And that it . . . was always gonna be like that." One day when she felt particularly isolated and alone, Moore grabbed a soda can and cut herself with the sharp edge. She experienced an almost immediate sense of relief. "I just remember kind of looking down and be like, 'I did that.' And I just remembered just having kind of this euphoric, everything's okay." Looking back now, Moore realizes that she never should have headed down the dark, dangerous path of self-injury. It quickly became her only way of coping with anything that went wrong in her life, even the smallest, most trivial problems. "It was, 'OK, I can cut myself. And it'll go away,'"[66] she says.

The Road to Recovery

Although Moore tried to keep her self-injury a secret from her parents, they could tell that something was not right. Her mother started to investigate, looking for clues about what might be wrong, and she found Moore's online journal and pages of bloodstained poetry she had written. One of Moore's poems was particularly chilling: "Can't take the anger, can't take the pain. Must relieve the only way I can. Cut. Cut. Cut."[67] Her parents found a therapist who understood self-injury, and Moore began to see her regularly. Guided by her therapist she slowly began to get better—and as that happened, her deep-seated need to cut herself began to fade.

Through therapy Moore learned that she was not a bad person, as she had believed for a long time. She also learned that when she was stressed or in pain she could use alternatives to cutting in order to feel better.

> " For the teen who has become accustomed to handling stress by cutting or self-injuring in other ways, the idea of giving up that behavior can seem unbearable— even impossible. "

Rather than hurting herself, for instance, she could take out her aggression on a desk or other nearby object. "I don't think I'll ever fully be able to say I'm completely done with it. It's completely over," says Moore. "But I'm at a point right now where I'm stable. I'm happy. I can function. So I'm pretty sure that this is where I'm gonna be."[68]

Tough to Quit

For the teen who has become accustomed to handling stress by cutting or self-injuring in other ways, the idea of giving up that behavior can seem unbearable—even impossible. It has become their go-to coping mechanism;

what they instinctively do whenever they feel stressed, frustrated, or are hurting. "You are asking them to change ingrained behaviors where they feel relief,"[69] says Tampa, Florida, psychotherapist Nancy Gordon.

Giving up self-harming behavior means acknowledging that it is an unhealthy and dysfunctional way of coping with life's problems. And then the person must truly want to stop self-injuring. "The child has to decide they're not going to do this anymore," says David Rosen. "Any ultimatum, bribery, or putting them in a hospital is not going to do it. They need a good support system. They need treatment for underlying disorders like depression. They need to learn better coping mechanisms." Rosen goes on to say that when teens decide to stop self-harming and then get stressed again, it is essential that they manage the stress in other ways. "They can't succumb to cutting," he says. "People who can figure out some alternative way to manage stress will eventually quit it."[70]

A young New York woman named Steph began to use cutting as her primary tactic for coping with fear and distress when she was fourteen years old. "It worked as a distraction for me," she says. "[Cutting] turned that more emotional pain into something tangible." Today thin scars cover Steph's legs and forearms. Even though a decade has passed since she cut herself the first time, she still struggles to control it. "It's a comfort in a twisted way. It really is," she says. "And it's really hard to stop."[71] Steph has made progress, however. At her worst point, when she was seventeen and living with her family in Fort Meyers, Florida, she was cutting up to ten times a day. Now she attends weekly therapy sessions and twelve-step meetings and has been able to go for nine-month stretches of time without cutting. Whenever she hears about or sees examples of other young people struggling with self-harm—on television or the Internet, for example—she finds it disturbing. "I wish I'd never started," she says. "And when I see other people who cut it makes me really sad for them. I think it's terrible."[72]

Essential Psychotherapy

Mental health specialists emphasize that teens who self-injure have emotional issues that they need help working out, and therapy can be invaluable for this. "Participating in therapy," says the Cornell Research Program on Self-Injury and Recovery, "can be useful in recognizing and acknowledging the importance of self-injury in a person's life, uncovering patterns of behaviors, identifying and recognizing triggers, learning coping skills, managing stress and learning to recognize and work with strengths." The Cornell group goes on to say that finding the right therapist can be challenging but is vital in order for the teen to overcome self-injury. "Most important is that the person find someone he/she connects with and, ideally, who can provide both support as well as challenge boundaries when needed. Finding someone who has experience working with individuals who self-injure is helpful but not critical."[73]

Depending on the patient's individual needs, several different types of therapy may be recommended. One that has been shown to work well with self-injuring teens is known as cognitive behavior therapy (CBT), which is a blend of two therapies: cognitive and behavioral. According to the National Institute of Mental Health (NIMH), cognitive therapy focuses on the patient's thoughts and beliefs and how they affect moods and actions, whereas behavioral therapy focuses on the person's actions. "CBT helps a person focus on his or her current problems and how to solve them," says the NIMH. "Both patient and therapist need to be actively involved in this process. The therapist helps the patient learn how to identify distorted or unhelpful thinking patterns, recognize and change inaccurate beliefs, relate to others in more positive ways, and change behaviors accordingly."[74]

> " Mental health specialists emphasize that teens who self-injure have emotional issues that they need help working out, and therapy can be invaluable for this. "

One form of CBT is dialectical behavior therapy (DBT), which has proved to be especially effective at helping teens overcome self-harming behaviors. At the root of this technique is the therapist working with the patient to help him or her learn how to tolerate uncomfortable feelings of anger, anxiety, and/or despair without resorting to self-injury. "The term 'dialectical,'" says the NIMH, "refers to a philosophic exercise in which two opposing views are discussed until a logical blending or balance of the two extremes—the middle way—is found."[75] A primary emphasis of DBT is the concept of validation, as the NIMH explains:

In keeping with that philosophy, the therapist assures the patient that the patient's behavior and feelings are valid and understandable. At the same time, the therapist coaches the patient to understand that it is his or her personal responsibility to change unhealthy or disruptive behavior. . . . The therapist consistently reminds the patient when his or her behavior is unhealthy or disruptive—when boundaries are overstepped—and then teaches the skills needed to better deal with future similar situations. DBT involves both individual and group therapy. Individual sessions are used to teach new skills, while group sessions provide the opportunity to practice these skills.[76]

Intensive Inpatient Care

Teens who are unable to break the destructive cycle of self-injury may need more intensive treatment, such as an inpatient program like S.A.F.E. Alternatives. Located in St. Charles, Missouri, S.A.F.E. therapists teach patients how to understand why they have negative feelings and then show them how to handle those feelings. At the heart of the S.A.F.E. philosophy is that if teens can succeed at making healthy choices, they will have no need to go back to self-harming. "I've been doing this for 20 years, and the success rate is far greater than the failure rate," says co-founder Karen Conterio. While acknowledging that not everyone who goes through the program succeeds at giving up self-harming behavior, "Others have finally decided to do the work they learned here. When they apply it, they do well. It all goes back to choice."[77]

> "Teens who are unable to break the destructive cycle of self-injury, may need more intensive treatment, such as an inpatient program like S.A.F.E. Alternatives.

Tara Prutsman, who started cutting herself when she was fifteen, had tried to stop self-harming on several occasions, but she always relapsed. Then she heard about S.A.F.E. Alternatives and decided to sign up for it. She spent two weeks as an inpatient and two weeks as an outpatient, and during that time was able to work through her emotional trauma and get her self-harming under control. "It's constant therapy and hard work," says Prutsman, but "it's worth it. I finished this past June, and I haven't hurt myself since. . . . So many self-injurers suffer alone because they're afraid to reveal their problem. I want people to know they can get help."[78]

Troubling Study Findings

When teens are interested in seeking help for cutting and other forms of self-injury, it is not uncommon for them to feel afraid and also uncertain about where to turn. Because of that, combined with the familiarity young people typically have with the Internet, an obvious starting place is the Worldwide Web—and according to a major study published in March 2014, this could lead to serious problems. The study was led by Stephen Lewis, a psychology professor at the University of Guelph in Ontario, Canada. Lewis and a team of graduate students had two primary goals: to learn how often people search online for information about self-injury, and to assess the quality of the available information. They used the Google AdWords Keywords program to identify ninety-two terms related to non-suicidal self-injury, limiting their search to those sites that receive at least a thousand hits per month. For each term the team focused only on the first page of websites displayed because, as Lewis explains, "often people don't get beyond that when doing online searches."[79]

> When teens are interested in seeking help for cutting and other forms of self-injury, it is not uncommon for them to feel afraid and also uncertain about where to turn.

During the study Lewis's team learned that there were more than 42 million unique searches for self-injury–related websites worldwide (based on the search terms used). Other findings were anything but positive. The researchers found that approximately 90 percent of the sites providing information on self-injury were either poor quality, not credible, and/or contained information that perpetuated harmful myths.

"Unfortunately," says Lewis, "much of the information we found on the Internet is of poor quality, and some of it propagates myths about people who self-injure, which may lead to further stigmatization and isolation." Lewis says that besides exposing people who self-injure to unreliable and inaccurate information, this also affects family members or anyone who is trying to help them. "Parents, peers, and others looking to help someone with NSSI may also be seeking information online, and what they are finding may be impacting their effectiveness as sources of support. . . . The Internet potentially is a powerful vehicle to reach out to those who self-injure and offer help and recovery resources. But we have to do it effectively and correctly."[80]

There Is Always Hope

Young people who have overcome the need to self-harm are usually the first to say that the road to recovery is not an easy road to travel. This is largely because self-injury is not just a bad habit. Rather, it is a way of life for teens who use it as their primary—and often only—method of coping with emotional pain, stress, and frustration. Still, many who have self-injured (even for years) have been able to beat the problem and go on to live happy, healthy lives free from self-inflicted harm. As one former self-injurer wrote in an online forum: "Recovery is a long hike, but do it anyway. The view from the top is amazing."[81]

Primary Source Quotes*

Can Teens Overcome the Need to Self-Injure?

66 Group therapy might be helpful in decreasing the shame associated with self-harm, and in supporting healthy expression of emotions. **99**

—Cleveland Clinic, "Self-Injury," February 4, 2014. http://my.clevelandclinic.org.

Located in Cleveland, Ohio, Cleveland Clinic is an academic medical center that integrates clinical and hospital care with research and education.

....

66 It's hard enough for a cutter to open up in individual and family therapy. To be expected to open up and share authentically in a group setting—usually in front of perfect strangers—is simply unrealistic. **99**

—April Kujawa, "Just Say No: Why Group Therapy Is Contraindicated for Self-Harm," Kahn Institute for Self-Injury, 2014. http://selfinjuryinstitute.com.

Kujawa is a fellow and intake coordinator at the Kahn Institute for Self-Injury.

....

* Editor's Note: While the definition of a primary source can be narrowly or broadly defined, for the purposes of Compact Research, a primary source consists of: 1) results of original research presented by an organization or researcher; 2) eyewitness accounts of events, personal experience, or work experience; 3) first-person editorials offering pundits' opinions; 4) government officials presenting political plans and/or policies; 5) representatives of organizations presenting testimony or policy.

66 Every time we hurt ourselves, we go backward in our recovery, not forward. 99

—Erin, "Consequences of Cutting: Why My 'Coping' Method Backfired," *Daisies and Bruises* (blog), September 2013. http://daisiesandbruises.com.

Erin is a young woman who started cutting herself when she was fifteen and now uses her writing to help discourage others from harming themselves.

66 It is possible to guide someone out of self-harming and prevent it from developing into an addictive, vicious cycle. 99

—Jane Smith, *The Parent's Guide to Self-Harm: What Parents Need to Know*. Oxford, UK: Lion, 2012, p. 18.

Smith is director of Anorexia and Bulimia Care, a charity in the United Kingdom that helps teens with eating disorders and those who self-harm.

66 A lot of people who self-harm don't ask for help. Why not? You might be aware that you have some serious problems, but don't feel that you can tell anyone—so you don't talk about it. 99

—Royal College of Psychiatrists, "Self-Harm," July 2014. www.rcpsych.ac.uk.

The Royal College of Psychiatrists is the United Kingdom's professional organization responsible for education and training as well as setting and raising standards in psychiatry.

66 Stopping self-harming behavior isn't easy, and it'll take time. 99

—Margarita Tartakovsky, "Helping Your Child Reduce Self-Harming Behavior," Psych Central, October 16, 2013. http://psychcentral.com.

Tartakovsky is associate editor for the online mental health resource Psych Central.

❝By far, the most effective treatment for adolescent self-harming problems is family therapy.❞

—American Association for Marriage and Family Therapy, "Adolescent Self-Harm," 2013. www.aamft.org.

The American Association for Marriage and Family Therapy is the professional association for marriage and family therapists.

❝Schools, parents, medical practitioners, and other youth serving professionals all have an important role to play in identifying self-injury and in assisting youth in getting help.❞

—Cornell Research Program on Self-Injurious Behavior in Adolescents and Young Adults, "About Self-Injury," 2013. www.selfinjury.bctr.cornell.edu.

Cornell Research Program on Self-Injurious Behavior in Adolescents and Young Adults conducts research on self-injury and provides resources and tools to individuals who self-injure and their loved ones.

Facts and Illustrations

Can Teens Overcome the Need to Self-Injure?

- According to a report published in the March 2012 issue of the medical journal *Child and Adolescent Psychiatry and Mental Health*, no treatments have been specifically evaluated for treatment of self-injury in adolescents.

- A 2014 study by researchers from Canada found that less than **10 percent** of websites providing information about self-injury are endorsed by health or academic institutions.

- According to Boston, Massachusetts, psychiatrist Mathilde Ross, most teens who self-injure outgrow the practice by the time they are in their twenties.

- Psychiatrists Claire M. Brickell and Michael S. Jellinek say that self-injury patients who also suffer from depression or anxiety disorders may benefit from medications that are designed to treat those conditions.

- According to Mental Health America, self-harming behavior often lasts for **5 to 10 years**, but can persist much longer without appropriate treatment.

- A March 2012 report published in the medical journal *Child and Adolescent Psychiatry and Mental Health* states that cognitive and behavioral therapies show the most promise in treating young people who self-injure.

Helping Teens Recover

Mental health specialists say that there is no treatment especially designed for teens who self-injure, but a number of options exist that can help young people overcome the need to harm themselves.

Treatment	Result
Psychotherapy (also called therapy or counseling)	Helps teens identify and manage the underlying issues that trigger self-injuring behavior, learn skills to better manage distress, better regulate impulsiveness and other emotions, boost self-image, improve relationships, and improve problem-solving skills.
Medications	Doctors may recommend prescription drugs for teens who suffer from depression, anxiety disorders, or other mental disorders commonly associated with self-injury. By treating these disorders, teens may feel less compelled to hurt themselves.
Psychiatric hospitalization	Teens who injure themselves severely or repeatedly may benefit from being hospitalized for psychiatric care in a safe environment that provides more intensive treatment.
Psychiatric day treatment programs	May be beneficial for teens who need intensive psychotherapy but do not require inpatient hospitalization.

Source: Mayo Clinic, "Self-Injury/Cutting," December 6, 2012. www.mayoclinic.org.

- According to researchers Patrick L. Kerr, Jennifer J. Muehlenkamp, and James M. Turner, in a small study of female hospital patients with borderline personality disorder, three-fourths of the women experienced a significant reduction in self-injurious behavior after being treated with dialectic behavioral therapy.

Healthier Ways of Coping

One of the most difficult aspects of giving up self-harming behavior is that by doing so, teens are also giving up their primary way of coping with stress or frustration, or any other kind of emotional turmoil. In order to recover, they need to adopt new ways of coping that do not involve hurting themselves. Shown here are some possibilities.

Alternatives to Self-Harming Behaviors
Accept reality and find ways to make the present moment more tolerable.
Identify feelings and talk them out rather than acting on them.
Distract themselves from feelings of self-harm; tactics include counting to ten, waiting fifteen minutes, saying "NO!" or "STOP!," practicing breathing exercises, journaling, drawing, thinking about positive images, and using ice and rubber bands to relieve the need to self-harm.
Stop, think, and evaluate the pros and cons of self-injury.
Soothe themselves in a positive, non-injurious way.
Practice positive stress management.
Develop better social skills.

Source: American Academy of Child & Adolescent Psychiatry, "Self-Injury in Adolescents," July 2013. www.aacap.org.

- A study published in March 2014 by Canadian researcher Stephen P. Lewis and colleagues found that information on websites offering health-related information about self-injury is not always up-to-date or entirely accurate.

- Through her extensive studies, Cornell University researcher Janis Whitlock has learned that most who self-injure are able to stop within **5 years** of finding healthier ways to cope with stress and emotional pain.

Perils of Relying on the Web

According to Canadian psychologist Stephen P. Lewis, most young people searching for information about self-injury rely on the Internet—and based on his own research, he finds that troubling. In March 2014 Lewis and his colleagues published a study that found the quality of self-harm–related websites to be poor, with fewer than 10 percent of sites endorsed by reputable health and/or academic institutions. Shown on this graph are some of the findings that most concerned the researchers.

Internet-Based Self-Harm Information Sites That Provide . . .

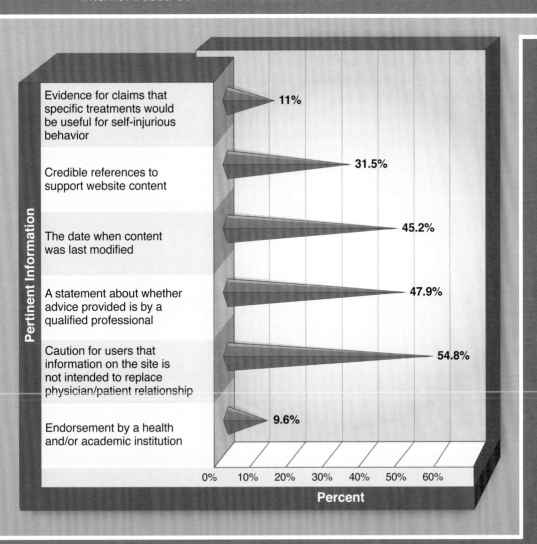

Pertinent Information	Percent
Evidence for claims that specific treatments would be useful for self-injurious behavior	11%
Credible references to support website content	31.5%
The date when content was last modified	45.2%
A statement about whether advice provided is by a qualified professional	47.9%
Caution for users that information on the site is not intended to replace physician/patient relationship	54.8%
Endorsement by a health and/or academic institution	9.6%

Source: Stphen P. Lewis et al., "Googling Self-Injury: The State of Health Information Obtained Through Online Searches for Self-Injury," *JAMA Pediatrics*, May 2014, pp. 443–49.

Key People and Advocacy Groups

Adolescent Self Injury Foundation: A nonprofit organization that provides education, prevention techniques, resources, research, and forums to help raise awareness about adolescent self-injury.

Karen Conterio and Wendy Lader: Nationally recognized experts on self-injury who cofounded the S.A.F.E. (Self Abuse Finally Ends) Alternative inpatient treatment program for self-injurers.

Cornell Research Program on Self-Injurious Behavior in Adolescents and Young Adults: A program affiliated with Cornell University that conducts research on self-injury and provides resources and tools to individuals who self-injure as well as their loved ones.

L. Eugene Emerson: A psychologist at Massachusetts General Hospital who in 1913 published the first known account of self-injury with his paper "The Case of Miss A."

Sharon Farber: A psychologist and author from New York City who specializes in self-injury.

Armando Favazza: A psychiatrist and author of the 1987 book *Bodies Under Siege: Self-Mutilation in Culture and Psychiatry*, which was the first in-depth psychological book about self-harm.

Michael Hollander: A psychotherapist who specializes in self-injury and is the author of the book *Helping Teens Who Cut*.

The Kahn Institute for Self-Injury: A group based in Los Angeles, California, that is devoted to the study and treatment of self-injury and offers support and treatment to self-injurers.

Marsha Linehan: A psychologist who developed the dialectical behavior therapy (DBT) approach to treating people with borderline personality disorder and/or those who self-injure.

Jennifer Muehlenkamp: An associate professor at the University of Wisconsin, Eau Claire, and a leading expert in self-injury.

Self Injury Foundation: A group that provides research funding, advocacy, support, and education for those who self-injure as well as their families and the health care professionals who work with them.

Barent W. Walsh: Executive director of the mental health facility The Bridge of Central Massachusetts, teaching associate in psychiatry at Harvard Medical School, and a renowned expert on self-injury.

Janis Whitlock: A psychologist, researcher, and founder/director of Cornell University's Research Program on Self-Injury and Recovery.

Chronology

1913
Self-injury first appears in medical literature with the publication of L. Eugene Emerson's "The Case of Miss A," an account of a young woman who repeatedly cut herself to relieve the pain of headaches; she was not mentally ill but had a childhood history of sexual and physical abuse.

1942
American psychologist Carl Rogers publishes *Counseling and Psychotherapy*, in which he suggests that a respectful, nonjudgmental approach to therapy is the most effective treatment of mental health issues.

1965
Researcher O. Ivar Lovaas and colleagues find that they are able to control the frequency of self-injury by manipulating social consequences: Positive reactions increase the frequency of self-injury, whereas ignoring the behavior decreases it.

1990
Ruta Mazelis, who specializes in self-injury disorder, develops and publishes *The Cutting Edge*, a newsletter that is targeted at people who are affected by self-injury.

1900   1970   1980   1990

1938
Psychiatrist Karl Menninger publishes *Man Against Himself*, a book that describes self-injury not as a suicide attempt but as a way to soothe oneself and an act of self-preservation.

1986
The Program for the Treatment of Self Injury is cofounded by psychotherapists Karen Conterio and Wendy Lader; its name is later changed to S.A.F.E. (Self Abuse Finally Ends) Alternatives.

1952
The first issue of *Diagnostic and Statistical Manual of Mental Disorders* (DSM) is published by the American Psychiatric Association, ushering in the formal classification of modern mental illnesses.

1987
Psychiatrist Armando Favazza publishes *Bodies Under Siege: Self-Mutilation in Culture and Psychiatry*, which is the first in-depth psychological book about self-harm.

1991
Psychologist Marsha Linehan publishes a paper about dialectical behavior therapy, a type of treatment that she developed for patients with borderline personality disorder as well as those who self-injure.

2006
Janis Whitlock and colleagues from the Cornell Research Program on Self-Injurious Behavior publish a study entitled "Self-Injurious Behavior in a College Population," which shows that one out of five college students have deliberately injured themselves at some point in their lives.

2013
The fifth edition of the *Diagnostic and Statistical Manual of Mental Disorders* is released; for the first time non-suicidal self-injury is listed as a recognized psychiatric condition.

2012
A study by four British health charities finds that among nearly fourteen hundred youth surveyed, more than half had self-harmed daily or a few times a week.

2000
In a revised edition of the American Psychiatric Association's *Diagnostic and Statistical Manual of Mental Disorders* the term *self-injury* is listed but only as a symptom of borderline personality disorder, not as a distinct condition.

2000

2010

1999
On March 1 the first Self-Injury Awareness Day is held; people throughout the United States and other countries widely distribute literature to help increase awareness of self-injurious behavior.

2007
After completing a study on self-injurious behavior, researchers from Harvard University and Boston University School of Medicine announce that the strongest factors in whether young people self-injure are sexual abuse and emotional neglect during childhood.

2009
The National Institute of Mental Health launches a study to compare the effectiveness of two treatments, dialectical behavior therapy versus a drug known as fluoxetine, for reducing the risk of self-injury and suicidal behavior in people with borderline personality disorder.

1995
In a BBC television interview Britain's Princess Diana discusses her private struggle in coping with severe emotional pain and reveals that she intentionally cuts her legs and arms.

2014
Canadian researcher Stephen Lewis releases a study showing that people seeking online help for cutting or other self-injurious behavior often receive incorrect or misleading information, with only one in ten websites endorsed by health or academic institutions.

Related Organizations

Adolescent Self Injury Foundation (ASIF)

11300 Rockville Pike
Rockville, MD 20852
phone: (301) 881-0433
e-mail: adolescentselfinjuryfoundation@gmail.com
website: www.adolescentselfinjuryfoundation.com

The ASIF is a nonprofit organization that provides education, prevention techniques, and other resources to help raise awareness about adolescent self-injury. Its website contains numerous facts about adolescent self-injury, tips on how to help others who injure themselves, and strategies to help teens refrain from self-harm.

American Academy of Child & Adolescent Psychiatry (AACAP)

3615 Wisconsin Ave. NW
Washington, DC 20016-3007
phone: (202) 966-7300 • fax: (202) 966-2891
website: www.aacap.org

Composed of nearly nine thousand psychiatrists and other interested physicians, the AACAP's members actively research, evaluate, diagnose, and treat psychiatric disorders. Its website contains a section titled Youth Resources that includes information for young people on coping with mental illness and finding help for themselves or their friends, as well as videos, a crisis hotline, and resources for families.

American Psychological Association (APA)

750 First St. NE
Washington, DC 20002-4242
phone: (202) 336-5500; toll-free: (800) 374-2721
website: www.apa.org

The APA is a scientific and professional organization that represents the field of psychology in the United States. Its website links to newspaper articles, research data, and a number of resources that focus on self-harm, stress, depression, and other related issues.

Cornell Research Program on Self-Injury and Recovery

Beebe Hall, Cornell University
110 Plantations Rd.
Ithaca, NY 14853
phone: (607) 255-6179
e-mail: info@selfinjury.bctr.cornell.edu
website: www.selfinjury.bctr.cornell.edu

Launched in 2003, the Cornell Research Program on Self-Injury and Recovery conducts research on self-injury and provides resources and tools to individuals who self-injure as well as their loved ones. Its website contains fact sheets, a blog, FAQs, a page of myths and facts about self-injury, an overview of recovery, and much more.

Kahn Institute for Self-Injury

6222 Wilshire Blvd., Suite 200
Los Angeles, CA 90048
phone: (323) 834-9641
website: http://selfinjuryinstitute.com

The Kahn Institute for Self-Injury, which is devoted to the study and treatment of self-injury, offers support and treatment to self-injurers. Its focus is looking at what needs to change in the family environment in order for the self-injurer to get better. The website provides information on self-injury and treatment, articles, and upcoming events.

Mayo Clinic

200 First St. SW
Rochester, MN 55905
phone: (507) 284-2511
website: www.mayoclinic.org

The Mayo Clinic is the largest nonprofit medical group practice in the world. Its website contains a section on self-injury and cutting that provides an overview of the symptoms, causes, risk factors, complications, coping tips, treatment, and prevention of self-injury, as well as information on offering support to those who self-injure.

Minding Your Mind

42 W. Lancaster Ave., 2nd Floor
Ardmore, PA 19003
phone: (610) 642-3879 • fax: (610) 896-5704
website: http://mindingyourmind.org

Through mental health education, Minding Your Mind works to reduce the stigma and destructive behaviors associated with mental health issues among adolescents and young adults. Its website provides information on news and events as well as numerous resources such as a section on mental health basics that includes facts, statistics, and information on early intervention.

S.A.F.E. Alternatives

4801 Weldon Spring Rd.
St. Charles, MO 63304
phone: (800) 366-8288 • fax: (888) 296-7988
e-mail: info@selfinjury.com • website: www.selfinjury.com

S.A.F.E. (Self Abuse Finally Ends) Alternatives is a world-renowned treatment program that has helped thousands of people stop self-injuring by empowering them to make healthy choices, including the choice to not self-injure. Its website offers a wealth of information, including news and events, webinars, a blog, FAQs, articles, and information on finding therapists and treatment centers.

Self Injury Foundation

PO Box 962
South Haven, MI 49090
phone: (888) 962-6774 • fax: (888) 296-7988
e-mail: info@selfinjuryfoundation.org
website: www.selfinjuryfoundation.org

The Self Injury Foundation provides funding for research, support, and education for self-injurers, their loved ones, and the professionals who work with them. The foundation's website contains information, news, and resources on self-injury, as well as a blog and a list of crisis hotlines and treatment centers.

Self-Injury Outreach & Support

website: http://sioutreach.org

Self-Injury Outreach & Support is a nonprofit outreach initiative run by a team of mental health professionals. It provides information and resources about self-injury to those who self-injure, those who have recovered, and those who want to help. Its website contains tips on learning to cope with the urge to self-injure, personal stories from people who have recovered from self-injury, and links to other organizations offering help to those who self-injure.

To Write Love on Her Arms (TWLOHA)

PO Box 2203
Melbourne, FL 32902
phone: (321) 499-3901
website: http://twloha.com

TWLOHA is a nonprofit organization that aims to help people struggling with addiction, depression, self-injury, and suicidal thoughts. The website contains a blog, mental health news, information on programs and events, an FAQ page, and links to helplines, counseling and treatment centers, and additional resources.

For Further Research

Books

Joan Esherick, *Suicide & Self-Destructive Behaviors*. Philadelphia: Mason Crest, 2013.

Sophia Gill, *101 Distractions from Depression, Self-Harm (and Other Soul-Destroyers)*, Kindle edition. Scotts Valley, CA: CreateSpace, 2013.

Melissa Higgins, *Teen Self-Injury*. Edina, MN: ABDO, 2014.

Greg Roza, *Cutting and Self-Injury*. New York: Rosen, 2014.

Cath Senker, *Self-Harm*. Chicago, IL: Heinemann-Raintree, 2012.

John M. Shea, *Self-Injury and Cutting: Stopping the Pain*. New York: Rosen, 2013.

Steven Smith, *Self Help for Self Harm*, Kindle edition. Seattle: Amazon.com, 2013.

Emily Stehr, *Knife Allergy and Treatment Plan: How I Didn't Cut My Throat, but I Did Cut My Forearm; My Journey Through Combat, Suicide, and Self-Harm*. Scotts Valley, CA: CreateSpace, 2013.

Lisa Verde, *How to Stop Cutting*, Kindle edition. Seattle: Amazon.com, 2014.

Jason J. Washburn, *Self-Injury: Simple Answers to Complex Questions*. Hoffman Estates, IL: Alexian Brothers, 2014.

Mary E. Williams, *Self-Injury*. Farmington Hills, MI: Lucent, 2013.

Periodicals

Lorenza Bacino, "Shock Figures Show Extent of Self-Harm in English Teenagers," *Guardian* (Manchester), May 20, 2014.

KJ Dell'Antonia, "A Son 'Cuts,' and a Father Struggles," *New York Times*, February 5, 2013.

Melissa Healy, "Self-Injury: Even Little Boys and Girls Do It," *Los Angeles Times*, June 11, 2012.

Lucie Hemmen, "Stressed Out Teen Girls: Cutting to Cope," *Psychology Today*, November 28, 2012.

Kate Hilpern, "Why Do So Many Children Self-Harm?" *Independent* (London), October 8, 2013.

Kay Lazar, "Cutting and Self-Injury Warning Signs," *Boston Globe*, March 12, 2013.

Kay Lazar, "Facing the Puzzling Urge to Injure," *Boston Globe*, March 11, 2013.

Brooke Magnanti, "Self-Harm May Be on the Rise, but It's Not All the Internet's Fault," *Telegraph* (London), May 23, 2014.

Ashley Mateo, "The Truth About Cutting: Why Stressed-Out Girls Are Taking Dangerous Measures to Cope," *Teen Vogue*, April 2014.

Radhika Sanghani, "Why Are More Talented Kids Self-Harming than Ever Before?" *Telegraph* (London), January 30, 2014.

Susan Seligson, "Cutting: The Self-Injury Puzzle," *BU Today*, April 3, 2013.

Stephanie Steinberg, "What to Do If Your Child Is Cutting," *U.S. News & World Report*, February 28, 2014.

Anna Stone, "Self-Harm: Why Would She Cut Herself?" *Telegraph* (London), October 2, 2013.

Sarah Vine, "My Chilling Journey into the Self-Harm Websites That Drove a Much Loved Daughter to Suicide," *Daily Mail* (London), January 17, 2014.

Alice G. Walton, "If Self-Injury Is So Prevalent, Why Do We Know So Little About It?" *Forbes*, January 31, 2012.

Internet Sources

American Academy of Child & Adolescent Psychiatry, "Self-Injury in Adolescents," July 2013. www.aacap.org/AACAP/Families_and _Youth/Facts_for_Families/Facts_for_Families_Pages/Self_Injury _In_Adolescents_73.aspx.

Marie Hartwell-Walker, "Teens Who Self-Harm," Psych Central, 2014. http://psychcentral.com/lib/teens-who-self-harm/0001962.

Rima Himelstein, "When Teens Cut Themselves," *Healthy Kids* (blog), *Philly.com*, April 29, 2013. www.philly.com/philly/blogs/healthy_kids/When-teens-cut-themselves-.html.

Raychelle Cassada Lohmann, "Deep Secrets: The Truth Behind Self-Harm," *Teen Angst* (blog), *Psychology Today*, October 14, 2012. www.psychologytoday.com/blog/teen-angst/201210/deep-secrets-the-truth-behind-self-harm.

Nadia Mendoza, "Inside the Mind of a Cutter: How Self-Harm Monopolised My Every Thought," *Huffington Post UK*, July 10, 2014. www.huffingtonpost.co.uk/nadia-mendoza/self-harm-recovery_b_5572097.html.

Jeannette Moninger, "Cutting: Why Teens Hurt Themselves," *Family Circle*, 2014. www.familycircle.com/teen/parenting/communicating/cutting.

Rick Nauert, "Being Bullied Increases Likelihood of Self-Harm," Psych Central, May 29, 2013. http://psychcentral.com/news/2013/05/29/being-bullied-increases-likelihood-of-self-harm/55357.html.

Melinda Smith and Jeanne Segal, "Cutting & Self-Harm," Helpguide, 2014. www.helpguide.org/mental/self_injury.htm.

TeensHealth, "Cutting," June 2012. http://kidshealth.org/teen/your_mind/mental_health/cutting.html.

Natasha Tracy, "Self-Injury Articles," Healthy Place, January 30, 2013. www.healthyplace.com/abuse/self-injury/self-injury-articles.

WebMD, "Teens, Cutting, and Self-Injury," 2012. http://teens.webmd.com/cutting-self-injury.

Source Notes

Overview

1. Quoted in Chloe Melas, "Sources Close to Demi Lovato Say She's Had an Eating Disorder & Cutting Issues for a Long Time," *Hollywood Life*, November 2, 2010. http://hollywoodlife .com.
2. Demi Lovato, interview by Kit Hoover, *Access Hollywood*, December 10, 2013. www.access hollywood.com.
3. Quoted in Rachel Ehmke, "What Drives Self-Injury and How to Treat It: Understanding Is the First Step," Child Mind Institute, March 5, 2013. www.childmind.org.
4. Timberline Knolls, "Self-Mutilation Symptoms and Effects." www.timberlineknolls.com.
5. Quoted in Samantha Gluck, "Teen Shares Self-Injury Secret," Healthy Place, July 5, 2013. www.healthyplace.com.
6. Quoted in Jeanie Lerche Davis, "Cutting and Self-Harm: Warning Signs and Treatment," *School Union Press*, June 24, 2014. www.schoolunionpress.com.
7. Emily, comment on Erin, "Consequences of Cutting: Why My 'Coping' Method Backfired," *Daisies and Bruises*, blog, September 3, 2013. http://daisiesandbruises.com.
8. Michèle Preyde et al., "Non-suicidal Self-Injury and Suicidal Behaviour in Children and Adolescents Accessing Residential or Intensive Home-Based Mental Health Services," *Journal of the Canadian Academy of Child and Adolescent Psychiatry*, November 2012. www.ncbi .nlm.nih.gov.
9. Janis Whitlock and Karen Rodham, "Understanding Nonsuicidal Self-Injury in Youth," *School Psychology Forum: Research in Practice*, Winter 2013. www.selfinjury.bctr.cornell.edu.
10. Whitlock and Rodham, "Understanding Nonsuicidal Self-Injury in Youth."
11. Quoted in Marie Hartwell-Walker, "Teens Who Self-Harm," Psych Central, January 30, 2013. http://psychcentral.com.
12. Quoted in Davis, "Cutting and Self-Harm: Warning Signs and Treatment."
13. Mayo Clinic, "Self-Injury/Cutting," December 6, 2012. www.mayoclinic.org.
14. Quoted in Davis, "Cutting and Self-Harm: Warning Signs and Treatment."
15. Quoted in Stephanie Steinberg, "What to Do if Your Child Is Cutting," *U.S. News & World Report*, February 28, 2014. http://health.usnews.com.
16. Marla Jo Fisher, "Teens Show Off Scars in Cutting's Pandemic of Pain," *Orange County Register*, April 8, 2014. www.ocregister.com.
17. Quoted in Davis, "Cutting and Self-Harm: Warning Signs and Treatment."
18. Quoted in Paul Burton, "Experts: Nearly 2 in 10 Teens Cut Themselves to Cope with Stress," CBS Boston, February 28, 2014. http://boston.cbslocal.com.
19. Office on Women's Health, "Cutting and Hurting Yourself," GirlsHealth.gov, October 31, 2013. www.girlshealth.gov.
20. Quoted in TheSite, "Long-Term Effects of Self-Harm," June 24, 2014. www.thesite.org.
21. Quoted in TheSite, "Long-Term Effects of Self-Harm."
22. Mental Health America, "Self-Injury." www.mentalhealthamerica.net.
23. Jill Emanuele, "Ask an Expert: My Daughter Who Is Self-Harming Has Agreed to See a Counselor. Is There Anything Else We Can Do?" Child Mind Institute, May 13, 2014. www .childmind.org.
24. Cornell University Research Program on Self-Injury and Recovery, "What Is Self-Injury?" 2013. www.selfinjury.bctr.cornell.edu.
25. Mayo Clinic, "Self-Injury/Cutting," December 6, 2012. www.mayoclinic.org.
26. Mayo Clinic, "Self-Injury/Cutting."

How Serious a Problem Are Cutting and Self-Injury Among Teens?

27. Raychelle Cassada Lohmann, "Teen Angst: A Silent Cry for Help: Understanding Self-Harm," blog, *Psychology Today*, February 28, 2012. www.psychologytoday.com.

28. Lohmann, "Teen Angst: A Silent Cry for Help: Understanding Self-Harm."

29. Quoted in Ryan Jaslow, "Self-Harm Study Finds Kids as Young as 7 Engage in Cutting, Hitting Themselves," CBS News, June 11, 2012. www.cbsnews.com.

30. Jennifer J. Muehlenkamp, Laurence Claes, Lindsey Havertape, and Paul L. Plener, "International Prevalence of Adolescent Non-suicidal Self-Injury and Deliberate Self-Harm," *Child and Adolescent Psychiatry and Mental Health*, March 2012. www.capmh.com.

31. Muehlenkamp, Claes, Havertape, and Plener, "International Prevalence of Adolescent Non-suicidal Self-Injury and Deliberate Self-Harm."

32. Muehlenkamp, Claes, Havertape, and Plener, "International Prevalence of Adolescent Non-suicidal Self-Injury and Deliberate Self-Harm."

33. Quoted in Lorenza Bacino, "Shock Figures Show Extent of Self-Harm in English Teenagers," *Guardian*, May 20, 2014. www.theguardian.com.

34. Quoted in Bacino, "Shock Figures Show Extent of Self-Harm in English Teenagers."

35. Quoted in Bacino, "Shock Figures Show Extent of Self-Harm in English Teenagers."

36. Whitlock and Rodham, "Understanding Nonsuicidal Self-Injury in Youth."

37. Janelle Harris, "Ignoring the Crisis of Cutting and Self-Harm Among Black Children," *Root*, March 1, 2014. www.theroot.com.

38. Harris, "Ignoring the Crisis of Cutting and Self-Harm Among Black Children."

39. Quoted in Selena Chavis, "Greater Risk for Self-Harm in Young Black Women," Psych Central, September 3, 2010. http://psychcentral.com.

What Causes Teens to Deliberately Harm Themselves?

40. Claire M. Brickell and Michael S. Jellinek, "Self-Injury: Why Teens Do It, How to Help," *Contemporary Pediatrics*, March 1, 2014. http://contemporarypediatrics.modernmedicine.com.

41. Raychelle Cassada Lohmann, "Teen Angst: Deep Secrets: The Truth Behind Self-Harm," blog, *Psychology Today*, October 14, 2012. www.psychologytoday.com.

42. Quoted in Ashley Mateo, "The Truth About Cutting: Why Stressed-Out Girls Are Taking Dangerous Measures to Cope," *Teen Vogue*, April 2014. www.teenvogue.com.

43. Quoted in Susan Seligson, "Cutting: The Self-Injury Puzzle," *BU Today*, April 3, 2013. www.bu.edu.

44. Quoted in Rick Nauert, "Being Bullied Increases Likelihood of Self-Harm," Psych Central, May 29, 2013. http://psychcentral.com.

45. Shavontaye Logwood, "Reader Submission: I Used to Cut Myself," *Gurl*, November 29, 2013. www.gurl.com.

46. Logwood, "Reader Submission: I Used to Cut Myself."

47. Quoted in Gary Warth, "Therapists See Alarming Growth in Teens Cutting Themselves," *San Diego Union-Tribune*, June 29, 2014. www.utsandiego.com.

48. Quoted in Warth, "Therapists See Alarming Growth in Teens Cutting Themselves."

49. Divya Kakaiya, "Guest Column: Self-Harming Teens Influenced by Social Media," *Pomerado News*, May 16, 2014. www.pomeradonews.com.

50. Anonymous, in Samantha Gluck, *Why Pro Self Injury, Pro Self Harm Websites Are Dangerous*, video, Healthy Place, August 24, 2012. www.healthyplace.com.

51. Quoted in Science Daily, "How Internet Affects Young People at Risk of Self-Harm, Suicide," October 30, 2013. www.sciencedaily.com.

What Are the Risks of Cutting and Self-Injury?

52. Mary L. Gavin, "Expert Answers On: Can a Person Get AIDS from Cutting?" Kids Health: For Teens, January 2012. http://kidshealth.org.
53. Quoted in TheSite, "Long-Term Effects of Self-Harm."
54. Quoted in TheSite, "Long-Term Effects of Self-Harm."
55. Erin, "Consequences of Cutting: Why My 'Coping' Method Backfired," *Daisies and Bruises*, blog, September 3, 2013. http://daisiesandbruises.com.
56. Whitlock and Rodham, "Understanding Nonsuicidal Self-Injury in Youth."
57. Erin, "Consequences of Cutting: Why My 'Coping' Method Backfired."
58. Kris, "I'm a Cutter. A Teenager Cutting Myself," Healthy Place, July 5, 2013. www.healthy place.com.
59. Kris, "I'm a Cutter. A Teenager Cutting Myself."
60. Quoted in Grace Macaskill, "Woman Who Almost Lost a Leg After Self-Harming with Biros Tells How She Conquered Her Demons," *Mirror*, February 22, 2014. www.mirror.co.uk.
61. Quoted in Macaskill, "Woman Who Almost Lost a Leg After Self-Harming with Biros Tells How She Conquered Her Demons."
62. Quoted in Ted Boscia, "Study: Self-Injury in Young People Is a Gateway to Suicide," *Cornell Chronicle*, December 4, 2012. www.news.cornell.edu.
63. Quoted in Boscia, "Study: Self-Injury in Young People Is a Gateway to Suicide."
64. Quoted in Michael Seamark, "My Precious Tallulah Was Lost in an Online World of Nightmares: Mother's Plea on Self-Harm Websites After Girl's Suicide," *Daily Mail*, January 22, 2014. www.dailymail.co.uk.
65. Quoted in Seamark, "My Precious Tallulah Was Lost in an Online World of Nightmares."

Can Teens Overcome the Need to Self-Injure?

66. Quoted in Gluck, "Teen Shares Self-Injury Secret."
67. Quoted in Gluck, "Teen Shares Self-Injury Secret."
68. Quoted in Gluck, "Teen Shares Self-Injury Secret."
69. Quoted in Mary Shedden, "The Unkindest Cut: Self-Harm About Relief, Not Suicide," *Tampa Tribune*, May 5, 2013. http://tbo.com.
70. Quoted in Davis, "Cutting and Self-Harm: Warning Signs and Treatment."
71. Quoted in Shedden, "The Unkindest Cut."
72. Quoted in Shedden, "The Unkindest Cut."
73. Cornell Research Program on Self-Injury and Recovery, "Professional Help," 2013. www .selfinjury.bctr.cornell.edu.
74. National Institute of Mental Health, "Psychotherapies." www.nimh.nih.gov.
75. National Institute of Mental Health, "Psychotherapies."
76. National Institute of Mental Health, "Psychotherapies."
77. Quoted in Davis, "Cutting and Self-Harm: Warning Signs and Treatment."
78. Tara Prutsman, "My Shameful Secret," *Cosmopolitan*, February 2008, p. 148.
79. Quoted in University of Guelph, "Study: Online Self-Injury Information Often Inaccurate," news release, March 31, 2014. www.uoguelph.ca.
80. Quoted in University of Guelph, "Study: Online Self-Injury Information Often Inaccurate."
81. Quoted in Celeste Pietrusza and Janis Whitlock, "Recovering from Self-Injury," Cornell Research Program on Self-Injury and Recovery, 2010. www.selfinjury.bctr.cornell.edu.

List of Illustrations

Index

Note: Boldface page numbers indicate illustrations.

Picture Credits

Cover: iStockphoto.com and Thinkstock/Comstock Images
SPL / Science Source: 11
Thinkstock Images: 17
Steve Zmina: 30–32, 44–46, 59, 60, 73–75

About the Author

Peggy J. Parks holds a bachelor of science degree from Aquinas College in Grand Rapids, Michigan, where she graduated magna cum laude. An author who has written more than a hundred educational books for children and young adults, Parks lives in Muskegon, Michigan, a town that she says inspires her writing because of its location on the shores of Lake Michigan.